THE WORKPLACE CURIOSITY MANIFESTO

THE WORKPLACE CURIOSITY MANIFESTO

How Curiosity Helps Individuals
and Workplaces Thrive in
Transformational Times

Stefaan van Hooydonk

"What I love with Stefaan's *Workplace Curiosity Manifesto* is that it makes clear and tangible how to unleash the unsuspected power of curiosity. Reading it enabled me to clearly see how to make curiosity a tangible and actionable pillar of growth for both individuals and organizations"

Thierry Debeyssac, Partner
Axialent

"*The Workplace Curiosity Manifesto* is a fantastic resource for anyone who wants to understand curiosity better and to hone the skill. It lays down compelling strategies to develop more curious people or 'A-players' for business owners & managers. A must read!"

Amit Garg, CEO
Upside Learning Solutions

"Excellent and clear. *The Workplace Curiosity Manifesto* helps you understand why curiosity is essential in a rapidly changing world. It helps individuals, teams and organizations succeed and thrive."

Ewa Hutmacher, CEO, co-founder
Snabbfoting Group AB

"I have found *The Workplace Curiosity Manifesto* a mandatory reading for those executives wondering how they can transform themselves and their teams. To my view, curiosity is the trigger of any wishing to increase effectiveness and team performance. Highly recommended."

Carlos Agustin Moreno, CEO
Grupo Altavista

"*The Workplace Curiosity Manifesto* is a unique and practical view into curiosity. As Stefaan says, it's a muscle that will be required for sustainable workplace success and can be developed intentionally."

Devendra Naik, Founder
NoMoBo Games

"A must-read for success in the 21st century. A thought-provoking and practical guide to meaningful growth through curiosity. If you're looking to transform yourself, your organization or our world, then I urge you to read this book."

Clare Inkster, Global Strategic planner
William Grant and Sons

'We are in dire need of asking different questions' - this is a phrase that jumped out at me from the pages of Stefaan van Hooydonk's delightfully provocative book. In a world crowded with life hacks and quick-fixes, here comes a pragmatic guide to rewiring the soul of the workplace conversation. This is not a guide to learning something new, but a window into the art of approaching the familiar without pretence of foreknowledge. Drink deep of this fount of wisdom!

Bijoy Venugopal, Director Corporate Communications
Flipkart

"I have found *Workplace Curiosity Manifesto* has become my go-to coach for triggering intent and action in my status quo mentality. Like me, anyone can learn to become a firestarter now."

Gurpreet Kalra, Head Talent Development (UK and Ireland)
Tata Consulting Services

"Heartfelt! This is an adorable work by Stefaan, sprinkled with a lot of gain and grain for your brain. It will compel you to nurture and nourish your curiosity for life. Soak into it to experience the sprouting up of your curiosity quotient and be convinced that personally or professionally, it's absolutely worth taking a curiosity risk!"

Sunil Tatkar, Founder and Managing Director
Valurevolution

"Reading *The Workplace Curiosity Manifesto* will provide you additional insights how curiosity is a personal and professional advantage, open you up to others in new ways and help you be prepared for all tomorrow will bring. No one knows what the next few years will bring, so sharpen your abilities to be curious and you will be prepared to take advantage of the opportunities to come."

William J. Ryan, Founder
Ryan Consulting

"The insights and tools described in the book lay a baseline for constant adaptability and life-long learning through the vector of curiosity - which means do not be afraid of failure because you are exploring, and the process of exploring is what is important. The chapters propose a great blend between definitions, theories and reflection questions that you can immediately use. A must read for anyone who thinks adaptability and transformation are and will be instrumental in our VUCA + environment."

Angela Feigl, Co-Founder and Lead Program Architect
DigitAll360

"Stefaan's *Workplace Curiosity Manifesto* has encouraged me to go beyond the obvious and dig deeper into what I can do as a leader to embody a growth mindset. It provides the case and tools for growing curious minds at scale – a must-read for organizations who wish to thrive in the complexity of the 21st century."

Anabel Dumlao, Partner
Axialent

"*The Workplace Curiosity Manifesto* is a testament of why curiosity should not be considered just some fad among learning and human capital professionals, but a trend that should be embedded into everything individuals, teams, and organizations believe in, say, and do. Van Hooydonk beautifully walks us through the philosophical, biological, psychological, and social evidence behind curiosity, laying out the differentiators that define A players and A companies. A must read for both curious and incurious leaders out there."

Dominik Rus, Global Head of Learning Technology and Innovation
TTEC

"This *Manifesto* is an amazing book. It offers a new body of knowledge. I'm convinced that we need to find ways to help employees flex their curiosity. Psychologists can benefit from these insights to improve their talent selection assessment process. We want people to ask big questions and we want to celebrate them when they do. We want them to think up experiments that haven't been done before."

Han van der Pool, Business Psychologist

"Curiosity is the new growth mindset. Stefaan's *Workplace Curiosity Manifesto* distills curiosity into its essence. Like Simon Sinek's why/how/what, it's a wonderfully simple, sticky concept, which makes it accessible and immediately beneficial to everyone. He gives us to the tools to harness and leverage our innate curiosity to improve professional performance, and businesses the tools to create a curious culture fueling innovation, create competitive edge and is core to the important topic of inclusion. Brought to life with stimulating examples, provocative thinking and compelling arguments this book will become your new binge series. When you do finally look up from this book you will find yourself seeing the world with entirely fresh eyes.

Rob Ferrone, Founder and Director
Quick Release

"Unlocking the next wave of innovation and growth will take leaders who are willing to expand their thinking about the big challenges. Stefaan's work is a vital reminder of the power of curiosity and an invitation embrace it in our organizations."

Sean Kennedy, Director of Expanded Education
Rhode Island School of Design

"We are in a time where re-thinking is central, work will never be the same, and I suggest we move from being people centric to person centric. The publication of: *The Workplace Curiosity Manifesto*, could not have been better timed. The lessons to take from the book are powerful."

Mille von Appen Hertz, People and Culture Wizard

"Curiosity is necessary for change in a world that requires more agility. Building a culture of curiosity becomes key for organizations to survive, and even thrive, through VUCA times. With Van Hooydonk's curious mind as North Star, this book explores and maps out the conditions necessary to embark on the journey. The different routes, of success and failure are underpinned by case studies that bring the various aspects to life and uncover the patterns to make curiosity a habit."

Gideon Lopes Cardozo, Agile lead of a large energy company

"Curiosity has a broad spectrum and each individual defines curiosity differently. I have found *The Workplace Curiosity Manifesto* amazing; it has identified so many different aspects to curiosity. Stefaan wonderfully captured the agents driving those curiosity triggers and what role as an enabler one can play in architecting curiosity dimensions. A fantastic read and a mind opener piece."

Divya Pareek, Learning and Performance Consultant

"Wow, a must-read for all who want to stay relevant and are humbly curious to explore new horizons. For me, this is such an encouraging manifesto filled with recognition, explanation, reasoning and way forward sparkles. On top, the inspiring content provides my curiosity muscle with nourishing food for reflection & discovery, new insights and … my internal idea generator got activated too!"

Henriette Wesselink, Senior Human Resources Consultant
Deutsche Telekom

"With this book, Stefaan has found the perfect mix of ideas, stories, and questions to get readers to rethink how they work, lead, learn, and even build relationships. Curiosity and talent development must go hand in hand to meet the needs of a rapidly changing world. Stefaan's book offers great new insights into how to do this."

Vincent-Pierre Giroux, Head of Talent Management, Americas
Alstom

"I have found *The Workplace Curiosity Manifesto* an exciting read, because it not only helped me to crack the nut why A-players are different than the rest, but even showed me ways to incorporate identification and development of curious people to the strategy of the company. The book is a must-have to anyone, who wants to build a successful organization in today's world."

Rob Byssz, Group Head of Transformation and Standardisation
Rohlik Group

"If you are *curious* to discover the difference between the 'A' and the 'B' players, and much more, please read this excellent book!"

Éric Saint Gelais, President
Miyagi Solutions

"Stefaan lucidly sheds light on the what, the why, and how of curiosity and gives a clear blueprint for professionals and organizations to embed it. With the book, you'll have strategies to thrive in the unprecedented times we live in."

Teena George, Founder
Habits and Mindsets

"*The Workplace Curiosity Manifesto* takes us through an inside-out journey, an exploration of what curiosity is, demystifies the curiosity code with definitions and sensitization with inspiring stories to trigger the inner curious agent to build a continuous curious journey at an individual and organization level.

A manifesto to ignite curiosity, enable mindset shifts, a new wave (ground breaking curiosity tsunami) and thinking transformation. Get crowned with curiosity!"

Melvin Errold Joseph, Deputy General Manager
Tractors and Farm Equipment Limited

"The one book that unravels curiosity and the business impact of the same. 'Surprise triggers questions and questions trigger curiosity. Curiosity triggers even more questions.' The book drives you towards an intentional mindset to challenge the status quo, explore, discover, and learn. A well-researched and fascinating read on Curiosity."

Natasha Jasrotia, Associate Director Learning and Development
Cognizant

"It is not always easy to penetrate the essence of something. And if it does succeed, it is often so simple and enlightening. As if you always knew. Only there was no one who just said it. Stefaan van Hooydonk has managed to touch an essence with this book: curiosity as a source of learning, development and discovery. Clearly written and practically applicable at every level in organizations and everyone's personal life."

Rolf Holtjer, Global Head Leadership Development
Rockwool

NEW DEGREE PRESS

THE WORKPLACE CURIOSITY MANIFESTO

*How Curiosity Helps Individuals and Workplaces
Thrive in Transformational Times*

ISBN

979-8-88504-141-6   *Paperback*

979-8-88504-774-6   *Kindle Ebook*

979-8-88504-253-6   *Digital Ebook*

To all curious professionals out there.

You are the real heroes.

CONTENTS

———

INTRODUCTION

──

"Curiosity has its own reason for existing. One cannot help but be in awe when one contemplates the mysteries of eternity, of life, of the marvelous structure of reality. It is enough if one tries merely to comprehend a little of this mystery every day."

—ALBERT EINSTEIN

When I was twelve, my sister made fun of me because I wanted to learn Sanskrit and was reading too many books. At fifteen, I took evening classes in modern Greek. When I was seventeen, I solo-hitched from my native Belgium to Greece and Turkey for two and a half months. I worked and lived in Hong Kong, China, France, Finland, Belgium, the Netherlands, India, Saudi Arabia, and the United Kingdom. I think I have always been a very curious person.

I started my professional career in investment consulting, then set up the executive education arm of a new business school in Shanghai. Subsequently, I set up corporate universities for Agfa, Nokia, Philips, Aramco, and Flipkart and was also the chief learning officer for Flipkart and Cognizant. In my last job at Cognizant, my team and I oversaw the growth and development of three hundred thousand employees globally. Amid the COVID-19 pandemic, I left my corporate role and founded the Global Curiosity Institute.

During my career, I had the privilege of working with many people. What struck me was, regardless of seniority, gender, background, religion, or any other differentiator, some people ask more questions than others. Such people are more interested in the world, others, and themselves. They consume more information, whether it is reading books or articles, viewing YouTube, or listening to podcasts or audiobooks. They also tend to spend more time getting to know new members of the team. They are not afraid to say they don't know something. I ended up calling these people "A-players." I only realized later their biggest differentiator was curiosity.

A-players differ from "B-players." B-players, too, want to grow and develop into a better version of themselves, only they have lost something along the way from early childhood until the present, something preventing them from going full out. B-players need someone or something to help them get going. In most organizations, A-players are in the minority.

This book is about curious people and the way they think, behave, act, and communicate. Though all of us are born curious, some have maintained stronger capacity for curiosity than others.

Curiosity is a muscle, just like any muscle in the physical body. The more we use it, the bigger and stronger it gets. Stop using it, and it atrophies, becomes weak, and is prone to damage. With the right insight about how to change and the right level of discipline and focus, we can all learn to become A-players.

We all have the power to show up curiously and even create curious environments. Curiosity thrives on intentionality. As such, it is more a verb than a noun; it requires intent, motivation, action, and perseverance. Those individuals and companies who embrace it proactively get results; those who take it for granted and leave it to chance don't reach their full potential.

The beauty is: we can stand on the shoulders of giants who have shown us the way. We only need to know how and where to look.

Curiosity is a powerful force. It is no wonder the World Economic Forum has placed curiosity on the top of their twenty-first century character traits list (Luo 2016). Curiosity is also a fragile thing. It needs both an intrinsic agent as well as a nurturing environment. In addition, it is fragile because the human species prefers predictability and the stability of the known world more than venturing out into the uncertain world of the unknown.

A crucial misconception is: curiosity will naturally occur in any reasonably healthy workplace. In fact, curious work environments are rare. They require deliberate and consistent action.

This book is a guide for anyone who wants to see what more they can do. Whether you are involved in operations, innovation, the people function, learning and development, marketing, or strategy, you will find inspiration in this book. Whether you are an executive or an individual contributor, you'll discover how to start questioning your underlying premises and how to take steps to move on the path of curiosity.

The Workplace Curiosity Manifesto is written for those curious minds who realize our lives, our teams, and our organizations (and ultimately our societies and planet) need the right adjustments to keep thriving.

You'll discover the stories of leaders, teams, and even organizations who naturally embody curiosity. Indeed, curiosity works at all these levels. Here are three short stories to get warmed up.

(1)

Jeltje Peletier is fifty-five years old and a Dutch citizen. Earlier in life, she studied Chinese in university, working for many years in international trading in Beijing and Guangzhou. When she and her husband started a family, she decided to quit her job and stay home.

When her children started to leave the parental nest, Jeltje decided to go back to work. At the age of forty-five, she went back to school to get a degree in psychotherapy. On top of that, she took extra courses to become a yoga therapist and a coach, which gave her extra tools to help the customers in her care.

What characterizes her after hundreds of hours of working with clients is she still carries with her a rare humility. She spends extra time studying the specifics of her clients' cases and goes out of her way to call fellow psychologists to discuss her cases. Her curiosity is driven from a place of thinking she can always do better; she does not know everything, yet wants to, and she puts in the time and energy in the pursuit of excellence.

(2)

A good engineer is someone who thrives on finding and solving difficult problems. Yet, how does one recruit the best of the best in a market where it is hard to tell good from average engineers, and where are there more job openings than engineers to fill them? The recruiting team at Google in Silicon Valley were asking themselves these specific questions. They needed to come up with something new, a new approach to recruit the best of the best.

To recruit the best—the most curious and problem-solving—engineers, they had to think of a radically new recruitment strategy. What they did was startling: they booked a large billboard on Highway 101 in Silicon Valley to display only this simple text:

> {first ten-digit prime found in consecutive digits of e}.com

The billboard had no company listed. Those who were curious and driven enough to find an answer to this puzzle would find themselves accessing the following URL: 7427466391.

com. Once they accessed the site, they would see yet another puzzle. Once they solved this second puzzle, they would get an invitation to fast track their application to problem-solver@google.com.

(3)

Fujifilm was hit equally hard as their competitor, Eastman Kodak, at the end of the twentieth century with declining sales. Both were supplying the entire world with photography film before digital cameras were invented. Both were very successful. As long as the market was stable and growing for most of the twentieth century, both Kodak and Fujifilm felt they were kings of the photography jungle. Once the crisis hit, their reactions in how to deal with it was, however, radically different from each other.

Even though Kodak had invented digital photography, their management failed to embrace this new technology. Deep down, they did not have the right mental models, humility, openness, and culture to let go of their lucrative legacy to reinvent themselves. Unbeknownst to them, while sitting on their cushy throne, they had gradually lost the initial impetus of their founder and became risk-averse, lost their capacity of listening to new market forces, were overconfident when faced with changes, and overall had lost their exploration mindset.

They were comfortable with the world they knew; anything beyond this known world was shielded from their radar.

Eastman Kodak's biggest rival was Fujifilm. They had also become big in the world of analogue photography and saw their sales drop drastically with the advent of digital cameras. Different from Eastman Kodak, they explored the application of their technology in radically different industries and listened to trends in not only the Japanese home market, but also other markets.

Fujifilm is thriving today because they faced their crisis with openness and curiosity. They also acted on their curiosity. Eastman Kodak, on the other hand, has virtually disappeared from the planet. Few people remember the power of a "Kodak moment." Eastman Kodak was punished for being incurious.

There are curious professionals, teams, and organizations, and then there are incurious ones. The three curious actors we just described benefited from high levels of openness and curiosity. They share a drive to action, an urge to explore the unknown, a hunger so big it overrides the desire for the coziness and conformity of their familiar world. They also had leaders, boards, corporate cultures, processes, and practices around them that allowed them to leave the beaten path and take the roads less known.

Their stories, mental models, systems, and processes are easy to replicate. With the right focus every professional, team, and organization can invite more curiosity and thrive.

Why Curiosity? Why Now?

All the businesspeople, academics, entrepreneurs, and corporate executives I interviewed for this book agreed curiosity is needed now more than ever. Old questions require new answers considering the changes we experienced in our industries and society. I would go one step further.

We are in dire need of asking different questions.

The industrial management models and theories we adopted worked well, for the most part, in the twentieth century. It worked well as long as the competitive landscapes and markets were stable and predictable. The downside of this model was: industrial stability leads to stagnation. Innovation was something that did not fit squarely in this model, as it represented change and some level of rupture with the past.

Companies open to uncertainty and willing to embrace curious employees will thrive if they aren't already. I call these curious companies. In curious companies, innovation and experimentation is proactively pursued. These companies adopt the right organizational mindsets, values, and culture and translate these in conducive processes and practices. Curious companies value, train, and reinforce curious leaders, attract the best talent, and can outpace competition. We can find curious companies in new and old industries, start-ups, scale-ups, traditional organizations, and small and big companies.

Congratulations if you are a curious professional and your organization supports curiosity! Beware, however, if your curiosity comes from a mindset of overconfidence: arrogance leads to a state of incuriosity. Ditto for organizations. Hubris leads to downfall.

The Harvard Business School professor Francesca Gino has written specifically about workplace curiosity in her *Harvard*

Business Review featured article in the September issue of 2018 titled: "The Business Case for Curiosity." We can distill three insights from her research into workplace curiosity:

1. Curiosity is more important to an enterprise's performance than was previously thought.

2. By making small changes to the design of the organization and the ways they manage employees, leaders can encourage curiosity and improve their companies.

3. Although leaders might say they treasure inquisitive minds, most in fact stifle curiosity.

We—including leaders—often attribute the positive effects of curiosity to ourselves, yet we tend to consider others in a more negative light.

At a societal level, there is indeed a love-hate relationship with curiosity. We link curiosity to scientific discovery, the joyous exploration of children, entrepreneurship, and success. At the same time, we also associate curiosity with inefficiency, gossip, and deviant, unruly behavior.

In my work with executives, 90 percent agree with this general statement: investing in curiosity to spark innovation is positive. When I zoom into their own teams, only 50 percent of these executives favor innovation. They worry curiosity leads to inefficiency and might distract the team from their focus.

Though workplace curiosity is hot these days, it is fragile and experiences many obstacles. The biggest hurdles to curiosity are stress and routine. It is not unexpected that the French existential philosopher Albert Camus cried,

> "Routine and pressure exhaust one's faculty of discovery and admiration."

The benefits of curiosity in the workplace are numerous. Curious employees are more engaged, more motivated, more open to changes, and volunteer novel ideas at work. Curious individuals also have greater willingness to try new things and see things from different perspectives. When the team is curious, we see reduced group conflict, less groupthink, fewer decision errors, and higher performance levels. Curious organizations see trends before others do and listen more deeply to market dynamics, customer needs, and the ideas of their employees. They innovate faster and are intentional about curiosity in their culture, processes, and practices. Curious organizations create the right environment for people to thrive. Curious companies are also magnets for the best talent.

Jeltje Peletier, Google, and Fujifilm are just three examples. Novartis, McKinsey, and PepsiCo are three more. Sber from Russia, Grundfos from Denmark, and Baobab Express from Africa are yet three more we will cover in this book. I could—and will—come up with lots more examples, yet I realize these individuals and companies are still the minority. No matter from where they hail, they all have something in common: curiosity about the world, others, and themselves.

And they are the opposite of their less curious peers.

What if we could all learn to be like those who inspire? I am confident we are at the brink of an era when the ability to inspire is practiced not just by the few, but by the majority. Studies show only a minority of our workforce shows up engaged at work. If more people knew how to improve themselves intentionally and how to build organizations that inspire curiosity, we would live in a world where the majority instead of the minority would be engaged and where companies would be more resilient in times of stress, more productive, and more creative. In such a system, employees also go home happier and build happier families.

This book is a tribute to all these professionals, teams, and organizations who are already showing up curiously. It is not designed to tell you what to do or how to do it. It attempts to offer you frameworks, inspiration, and a mental model for deciding to take action.

This book is a manifesto and, as such, calls for action in response to a challenge.

I offer you one now. From now on, don't be simply curious, be intentionally curious.

Before we dive in, I want to leave you with some initial questions to reflect on:

- Who is your role model when it comes to curiosity?

- When was the last time you learned something new to the point you could teach it to someone else?

- What is your definition of curiosity?

- To what degree do your colleagues consider you to be someone who is interested in novel things?

- To what extent is curiosity stimulated by your organization, your manager, your team, or your customers?

PART ONE

CURIOUS ABOUT CURIOSITY

1

DEFINING CURIOSITY

"It was a bright cold day in April, and the
clocks were striking thirteen."

—GEORGE ORWELL

This is the opening sentence of George Orwell's masterpiece
1984. Let's look at this sentence again.

"It was a bright cold day in April, and the clocks were striking *thirteen.*"

Consciously or not, a normal reader would immediately recognize a gap between normality and its opposite: abnormality.
Abnormality creates surprise. Surprise makes us want to learn
more. Scientists have dubbed this "information-gap theory."
The information-gap theory posits when someone has a gap
in their knowledge on a topic they care about, they will take
action to find out what they miss.

Clearly, we don't suspect analogue clocks in Orwell's time
to strike thirteen, so the unconscious frustration with what

we know is true (the max for a clock to strike is twelve) and the different information presented to us creates the perfect hook to dig deeper and start exploring the world of George Orwell's masterpiece. Surprise triggers questions and questions trigger curiosity. Curiosity triggers even more questions.

Maybe you are suddenly wondering about the meaning of the old proverb "the thirteenth stroke of the clock." It means all previous events or "strokes of the clock" must be called into question. Appropriately, curiosity does this very well. When we are surprised, we compare new information against the truths we hold to be self-evident.

Is surprise the only trigger to curiosity, or is there more to it?

Curiosity has been long considered as a mental power associated with imagination and creativity—with artists, inventors, explorers, and scientists. More recently, we have collectively realized curiosity is something driving progress for every single individual. Indeed, when we are curious, we view tough situations more creatively and are less defensive to the reactions of others, stress, or provocation. We perform better and are more engaged. When we are curious, we also learn better, faster, and deeper.

When I founded the Global Curiosity Institute, one of my first actions was to create the perfect definition of curiosity—one relevant for both individuals as well as larger systems: teams, organizations, and even society. To arrive at a workable version, I looked at the research, read philosophers, and talked to many smart people. In the last eighteen months, I have asked hundreds of people what their definition of curiosity is.

What became apparent quickly is curiosity does not let itself be contained in a unidimensional definition. Curiosity has a broad spectrum. On the one hand, it refers to many of us reacting to a beep on our smartphones. On the other hand, it explains Einstein's drive to understand something vast like the universe. Curiosity is linked to a negative behavior like gossip and, at the same time, is the driver for sending an exploration vehicle to the planet Mars.

What is your own definition of curiosity?

We all have our intuitive definition of curiosity. When gently pressed, we all can come up with our own intuitive definition of curiosity. The definitions I collected in interviews, workshops, and discussions with people are (in no particular order):

- Opening up to the wild unknown

- The fuel to adapt and be agile

- The energy, interest, desire, and knowledge to dig in to know more

- The drive to learn new things

- Challenging the status quo

- What kids do

We link curiosity to the joyous exploration of kids, the wonder we have about the world, the excitement of traveling to a new place, and many inventions, such as creating fire, the self-driving car, and so much more. In the workplace, we often link curiosity to new innovations, winning deals, understanding customers, and creative individuals. The attributions are mostly positive, but sometimes less positive.

Curious people learn faster and are more interested, engaged, and productive. The negative side of curiosity is people think it leads to inefficiency: too much thinking, too little doing. Some leaders think curious people are harder to manage.

If you are like me, a couple of years ago, you probably never thought about a definition or deeper meaning about curiosity. We take curiosity for granted. Curiosity is such a basic component of our nature; we are nearly oblivious to its presence and persistence in our lives. Consider how much of our daily efforts are spent engaging in activities not related to sleeping, eating, or mindless routines. It is hard not to be curious. We are constantly communicating with ourselves and others, searching for and consuming information, glancing at headlines, or listening to the news. We browse the internet in search of information or simply to kill boredom, listen to music or podcasts, or watching television, movies, and sports.

As with all things, once we start exploring curiosity beyond its superficial surface, we encounter hidden aspects we did not think about as well as a level of complexity we did not expect initially. This becomes immediately clear when we look at the definition of curiosity according to the online *Cambridge Dictionary*.

1. An eager wish to know or learn about something

2. Something that is interesting because it is rare and unusual

The above definition links to our intrinsic desire to know and learn more. At the same time, it also uncovers a different dimension, one where curiosity is aroused when we are surprised and when things are different from what we are used to. We'll come back to this.

The definition from the *Cambridge Dictionary* falls short of the multifaceted nature and complexity surrounding curiosity researchers have uncovered. Most of the definitions we find in dictionaries or the ones that are volunteered by individuals refer to intellectual or cognitive curiosity. In a few rare cases, like when I interviewed executive coach and culture specialist Teddy Frank, the definition goes further. She defines curiosity as "the intersection between our interest in the world, others, and ourselves." When reflecting a bit deeper, Teddy Frank's definition makes sense and fits squarely into my own model.

Beyond trying to understand the world, curiosity also refers to our empathic nature, our interest in bonding with other individuals. Additionally, it also covers our desire to explore the depths of our own personalities when we try to understand our own individual deeper drivers of our behavior or to articulate our individual values.

A FIRST WORKING DEFINITION

Defining curiosity is proving a bit harder than we originally thought, yet not impossible. Once we start to peel curiosity like the proverbial onion and look at different layers, we get exposed to its richness and potential for individuals, organizations, and societies. Curiosity drives learning, exploration, innovation, relationships, and understanding about ourselves.

Elliott Masie, a celebrated Broadway producer and long-term authority on corporate learning, shared his definition with me.

Curiosity is a form of hunger for knowledge, for context, for content, for solutions, and in some cases, even a hunger for other questions, a hunger for curiosity, if you will. It is a critical and often ignored component of how people learn, how they live, how they interact, how they solve, how they grow, even how they fail. I think we are driven in so many ways by curiosity. It motivates us, it moves us toward knowledge, toward activity, toward relationships.

Curiosity is related to whatever our tribal state is. My curiosity is different if I am living in a large metropolitan industrial area, working in a corporation or if I am a farmer in Cuba. It is very different if I am at a point in my life when I am a student seeking certification versus someone who is ill, who is figuring out how to get better. Curiosity is contextualized by its tribe. It shows itself differently at different times in different cultures. And even there are subcultures where curiosity is highly valued, or it is considered dissonance and disrespectful to be curious.

There is so much to unpack in Mr. Masie's definition. I suggest you reflect on it for a few moments. It will resonate throughout this book.

The definition I chose, one proven to work with individuals, teams, and organizations is the following:

Curiosity is the intentional mindset to challenge the status quo, explore, discover, and learn.

Allow me to explain these terms.

- **Intentionality.** Curiosity is something we do actively. It is like a verb; it assumes agency and choice. We choose to be curious (or not). Nobody is curious all the time. Some of us are curious at work, while at the same time incurious at home. Curiosity is like a muscle: it is something we can improve on or otherwise diminish its force when we don't train it properly and proactively.

- **Challenging status quo.** Curiosity is all about questioning the underlying status quo and asking pointed questions about the world, others, and oneself. It is about never being fully happy with standing still. Challenging the status quo does not have to be something reserved for only outgoing extroverts. It also means to question the merit of underlying hypotheses we ourselves or others might have about a situation or a customer, or when we start a new project.

- **Explore and discover.** These verbs are both the initiators of curiosity but can also be seen as the results of their respective actions. At a basic level, to "explore" means to search and is an intellectual (e.g., Einstein) or physical (e.g., Columbus) activity. It refers to something broad. It also creates hope as it might lead to something, but not necessarily does so. As we will see, exploration is the opposite of conformity. "Discovery" refers to something specific and narrower. One explores the streets of London, and one discovers a great museum. One explores ways to improve the way elderly citizens in elderly homes are treated and discovers new solutions to make their lives more comfortable.

- **Learning.** Learning consists of the acquiring of new knowledge, skills, behaviors, or mindsets as well as their result. The moment we stop being curious, we stop learning. As we will see, the inverse is also true. When we stop learning, we stop being curious. This is true not only for individuals, but also for teams, organizations, and even societies.

THE OPPOSITE OF CURIOSITY: CONFORMITY

Curiosity challenges the status quo and the desire to prefer a comfortable past over an uncertain future. Conformist behavior makes us want to stick to proven patterns of the past. Large systems like societies and companies or smaller systems like individuals are constantly trying to strive toward a state of conformity. Conformity gives us a feeling of certainty and stability.

Professor Edward Hess, professor emeritus of business administration at the Darden School of Business, underscored this beautifully to me: "If you look at children, you immediately see they like to explore, they are not fearful, they are more resilient. It is innate in them. It is, however, societally and educationally not sufficiently enhanced, enabled, and rewarded. Children lose their curiosity when their view of the world solidifies. At that moment, they seek confirmation of what they believe; they want to be liked by others, they want to be part of the in-crowd, they are raised not to make mistakes. For an adult to be genuinely curious, there must be something in place to overcome the societal, cultural, as well as one's own internal wiring."

As human beings, we are a confirmation- and stability-seeking species. We prefer the safety of the known world over the danger of the unknown. We favor light over darkness. We prefer to see the beliefs we have of the world and people around us confirmed rather than challenged.

Complacency and routine hamper our ability to be curious. Over the years, we lose our natural capacity to be intrigued by the mundane. We don't stop when we see a single white pebble amidst thousands of black ones like when we were young. Routine and monotony gradually kill curiosity.

The longer we engage in the same task and the same role at work, the more we become "part of the furniture" and stop asking the much-needed questions to improve. It stops us from challenging the status quo and innovating. We get used to the upward curve in the carpet. After a while, we take it to be normal. As I will share in more detail later, my research has found people who stay more than three years in the same role see a decrease in their individual curiosity levels.

Curiosity is the counterforce to overcome the gravitational pull of conformity. Too much conformity stifles us to a point where we don't want to try new things, ask new questions, visit new places, or get to know new friends. A little bit of curiosity helps us explore our current world. When we exert more than a little effort, we start to discover entirely new things we did not know existed before. As we shall see in the next chapter, this is the difference between narrow and broad curiosity.

When we encounter something or someone we don't know or that goes against our beliefs or experiences, we react with surprise. A little bit of stress is almost always uplifting, but too much of it kills curiosity and can be paralyzing. A knock on the door on a sunny afternoon can prompt multiple reactions. It can create a smile on our faces when we know a dear friend is likely to be standing outside. It can also be an agonizing event if one finds oneself in a war zone and enemy soldiers are visiting all houses in the city, looking to take prisoners. When the surprise is just right, it leads to magic. When that happens, we start to learn, to discover, and to explore.

Professor Kashdan, professor of psychology at George Mason University, mentioned a telling example of conformity: According to his research, couples who break up rarely do so because they are fighting. Most couples break up because they are bored with each other. They take each other for granted and stop exploring.

A small experiment will prove the fact we prefer to stay in the comfortable middle and typically do not prefer to look for extremes. At Starbucks, people have the choice between a small, medium, or large serving of their favorite beverage. Presented with these options, most people order the safe middle option: not too big and not too small. Once Starbucks introduced a fourth mega-big bucket-size option, suddenly the large option did not seem so extreme anymore (De Morgen 2022).

We are also good at looking for feel-good answers to questions rather than accurate ones. We often assign the wrong causation when confronted with issues. At such moments, it is harder to engage in "what if" or "why" thinking.

Shop owners are often averse to local governments trying to turn their shopping streets into pedestrian-only streets.

These shop owners worry that by inhibiting cars, customers have a harder time visiting their premises, and sales might drop. The reality shows them wrong. Shops thrive more in pedestrian-only streets than in streets where there is parking space. Cars don't shop, people do.

Conformity is not necessarily bad as it provides us with clarity about the rules of engagement, certainty, and predictability in our lives. Since the dawn of time, our ancestors' brains were hardwired for worry—worry to fit in our social group or worry to be eaten alive by a saber-toothed tiger. To help ourselves live through the day, we adopted a mindset to prepare for the worst and created strategies and routines to minimize threatening events.

This is also true in our workspaces. We require routines, processes, and practices to get things done at work. Without them, we would have to reinvent the way we work daily. The challenge starts when we only focus on following processes and stop asking questions, when we implement without thinking. In such workplaces, it is hard to go against the flow and suggest obvious changes. The US economist John Kenneth Galbraith said:

"In any great organization it is far, far safer to be wrong with the majority than to be right alone" (Burgers 2008).

Apart from worry, our ancestors were also endowed with curiosity, and so are we, especially in moments when we feel safe and there is no danger that things go wrong or that we look foolish in the eyes of others. In such rare, free moments, we are ready to explore new things and seek out new experiences.

In a work environment, when we think of the juxtaposition of curiosity and conformity for modern-day organizations, we can draw on the knowledge from the scientific innovation literature. There we can find analogies between the concepts of exploration and exploitation (Gupta 2006). Exploitation refers to implementing something in the most efficient way repeatedly. Exploration, on the other hand, refers to innovating, experimenting with the new. Start-ups are often high on exploration. Yet after a while, they become rigid and obsessed with exploitation at the expense of exploration in their drive toward operational excellence.

We will come back to this concept later. What I want to stress now is: it is not an either/or game. It is an and/and game. To be successful, individuals and organizations need both.

ARE CHILDREN MORE CURIOUS THAN ADULTS?

We know intuitively that children are curious, yet how do they react to conformity? Is curiosity a stronger or weaker sensation for infants when compared to conformity?

Susan Hespos, professor of cognitive psychology at Northwestern University in the United States, has been researching this question. To baseline the interest of infants, she has been measuring the length of time young children keep their focus while looking at an object in front of them. She found infants are twice as interested in novel and unpredictable images and situations than in predictable ones. The stranger the situation is, the longer they are intrigued. The more familiar the situation the quicker they become bored. This would indicate that, at least in young children, the curiosity trigger is in fact higher than the desire for conformity (Benstead 2020).

What researchers have found with regard to the high curiosity levels of children as compared to adults is children are not more curious than adults. The differentiator between children and adults is children—including adolescents—are willing to suffer more and take more risks to get access to the knowledge they desire an answer for (Dobbs 2011). This explains why children are willing to touch something hot, even when they have been warned doing so can cause pain. Adults, even when they are also curious, are not willing to go that far in the pursuit of knowledge. They assume their past routines and experiences help them to make sense of the world.

The same goes for question strategies. Children ask more "why" and "how" questions than adults do. They also ask more questions. Research by Dr. Sam Wass with 1500 families in the United Kingdom found young children are asking on average seventy-three questions a day (Steingold 2017). When we compare this to question strategies of teenagers, the number of questions drops to single digits. For the adolescent demographic, the quantity and quality of questions depends on whether asking questions is seen as positive in the peer group. When they enter the world of work, adults often limit themselves to functional questions, such as what do they need to do to stay out of trouble. "Why" and "how" questions are often not considered as a valid strategy at that point.

CURIOSITY KILLED THE CAT

Language has an enormous influence on how we view the world and reflect about it. Within and across cultures, the words and phrases used to describe curiosity range from positive to negative. At a deeper level, curiosity is a creative form of knowing.

It is undisciplined and does not let itself be confined. In curious environments, there is freedom to ask questions, even difficult and open-ended ones. The answers to such questions are not predetermined. This is one of the reasons why curiosity is perceived as being unruly in conformist organizations. In such environments, curiosity is not an item in the interviewing process.

In the Polish language, there is a saying: "Curiosity is the first step to Hell." In my opinion, this refers to an underlying moral statement, namely curiosity is unruly, leads to trouble, and should be avoided. I wonder if this saying comes from Poland being a very Catholic country, and the influence of a church that, for a long time, discouraged asking questions or engaging in independent thought.

In most of history, education, governments, and religion have heralded a similar message. Comply and you will benefit; don't and you will suffer.

The juxtaposition of conformity against curiosity is a modern concept where curiosity has the positive upper hand. Throughout the ages, curiosity was conceptualized in a myriad of ways. In most cases, curiosity had the underhand and was seen as disruptive and undesirable.

This insight led Ian Leslie, author of *Curious*, to conclude:

> For most of Western history, curiosity has been regarded as, at best, a distraction, at worst a poison, corrosive to the soul and to society.
>
> —Ian Leslie

Luckily, at present, in the professional sphere, especially in knowledge-intensive environments and increasingly in blue-collar environments, curiosity is fashioned as a positive trait for professionals.

The phrase "curiosity killed the cat" implies curiosity is hazardous, and those engaging in it are prone to risk taking and exploration. This common expression serves as a warning against inquiry; it is best to conform and stay quiet rather than explore novelty. In his 2017 book *Why?* the astrophysicist-turned-writer Mario Livio describes eloquently that this sentence was originally different. Its earlier version appearing in print at the end of the sixteenth century was "care killed the cat." "Care" in those days meant worry.

At the end of the nineteenth century, "care" was replaced by "curiosity," though it's not clear who started this change or why it was enforced. Not everybody agreed with this change, it seems, and to compensate for this negative shift, "curiosity killed the cat" was made longer with the positive add-on: "but satisfaction brought it back," probably as a reminder that curiosity still remains a key driver for the acquisition of knowledge (Livio 2017).

If you are interested in learning more about the history of the concept of curiosity, you can read about it in the bonus chapters you can find on: www.globalcuriosityinstitute/theworkplacecuriositymanifesto.

Interestingly, I became aware of an extra connotation of curiosity to cats when I spoke to Nick Shackleton-Jones, UK-based corporate learning consultant and author of *How People*

Learn. When I asked him about his curiosity, he said he got his own curious mind probably from…his cat.

Jokes aside, he explained one-third to one-half of the world population carries the parasite Toxoplasma gondii. Cats get it by eating rats. Humans get it from their cats. The parasite in rats reprograms the rats to head in the direction of risk instead of running away from it. As a result, they run toward their lethal enemies and get eaten. Nick Shackleton-Jones mentioned: "It has been thought the parasite was benign in humans, but it turns out, those people infected with toxoplasmosis are more likely to be risk takers."

This sounded too curious to be true, but some further research proved him right. People with toxoplasmosis are 2.65 times more likely to be involved in traffic accidents because—according to the research—they have impaired psychomotor performance or an enhanced risk-taking personality profile (Webster 2013).

Interestingly, agency influences how we define curiosity. When we think about ourselves as curious agents, we often consider its more positive aspects. When we think of others in relation to curiosity, we are suddenly not sure anymore.

DO SCIENTISTS AND ARTISTS PERCEIVE CURIOSITY DIFFERENTLY?

In common culture, the heroes of curiosity are scientists and artists. When thinking of science, names like Albert Einstein, Marie Curie, and many others are praised for their intellectual curiosity as well as their intrinsic drive to solve fundamental questions. Artists, too, are celebrated as curious role models. One only must think of people like Leonardo da Vinci, Jackson Pollock, or J.K. Rowling to see how their curiosity pushed them to explore new artistic horizons (and often themselves in the process).

I wanted to investigate how scientists and artists perceive curiosity. Do they view curiosity through the same lens or is it a different dimension altogether across the scientific and artistic spectrum? To find out, I spoke to Reynier Peletier, professor of astrophysics at the Groningen University in the Netherlands, and Soren Meibom, a Danish artist living in the USA. Interestingly, Soren Meibom holds a PhD in astrophysics too. Prior to choosing to become an artist, he had a successful research career as an astronomer and lecturer at the Harvard-Smithsonian Center for Astrophysics in Cambridge, Massachusetts.

In reflecting on curiosity, both individuals were not completely divergent, yet some interesting differences can be deduced.

Professor Peletier shared, "The role of intellectual curiosity in science is deeply rooted. One of its characteristics for curiosity is it needs to be in synchronization with intent and persistence to achieve results."

In his field of astrophysics, the stages of exploration of the universe have been guided by developments in technology. Whereas until the 1950s, when scientists were looking at the skies with telescopes, research has shifted to analyzing radio waves, X-rays, gamma-rays, and infrared to gather new data about the universe. According to him, the availability of new data has led to new questions and new answers. "The fact technology has evolved so much means scientists constantly need to be open to exploring new dimensions of space exploration. While the scientific method requires rules, boundaries, and accountabilities, there is still lots of room for exploration in our field." The challenge now, he shared, is "we have covered all wavelengths to gaze at the universe. A need is emerging for a new paradigm to study the universe, one with new questions and new answers."

Soren Meibom—a professor turned artist—agrees with this statement, yet he goes one step further. He uses the metaphor of scientific research being like rafting on a fast-flowing river. It is super exciting, fast-moving, and there are lots of things to explore, but much like science has rules and conventions to ensure high quality and the adherence to the scientific method, the river has banks and rocks and trees that will confine and obstruct you and possibly tip your boat upside down. In the world of art, according to Soren Meibom, those boundaries and rules are mostly gone. Creating art is more like an ocean on which your curiosity and creativity can sail you in any direction at any speed. However, that freedom can also be disorienting if your intellectual curiosity is not helping you set goals and destinations.

The world of workplace curiosity is somewhere on a scale in-between the world of science and art. We will discuss the traits of workplace curiosity in much more detail. What is important for now is to recognize the occupation we engage in professionally directly influences our definition of curiosity. Corporate executives, for instance, have a different perspective of curiosity compared to the employ-ees in their care.

Now that we are starting to see the broad contours of curios-ity, I suggest we take a step back and look at traits of curious professionals. Through the eyes of curious professionals—the A-players—we will see curiosity is, in fact, hiding an exciting complexity. We will explore further the depths of curiosity and discuss the difference between narrow and broad curiosity as well as productive and unproductive curiosity. We will also talk about why curiosity is not only a fixed trait remaining with us throughout life, but it is also dependent on our evolving state of mind. As we shall see, this is good news, as it empowers us to get constantly better at curiosity.

The Big Ideas

Though curiosity is a simple word we use loosely, it hides a myriad of aspects. The more we are aware of these differences, the more we are invited to become aware of our individual curious mindset and reflect on the curiosity predispositions in our organizations.

The opposite of curiosity is conformity. We are a confirmation-seeking species. We feel safe when we are in our comfort zones. However, this safety limits our growth. We often prefer the certainty of the known world to the unpredictability of what could be. Stress and routine enhance our desire to favor conformity. Only with intentional effort can we overcome the gravitational pull of conformity.

Language and culture explain why we have a love-hate relationship with curiosity. In all (sub)societies, we can distill positive and negative connotations of curiosity. It depends on which one of the two we choose as the dominant narrative for ourselves or our social group, family, or company. Having a positive or negative connotation, or where we stand and sit professionally, greatly influences how we perceive it and act upon it.

Questions for Reflection

- Did your original definition of curiosity change when reading this chapter? How?

- How do you know when you are showing up curiously (or not)?

- How well is curiosity accepted in your organization, family, and community?

- How different do you think workplace curiosity is from scientific and artistic curiosity?

- How intentional is your curiosity?

2

ARE YOU AN A-PLAYER?

"Open the window, there is a big world out there."
—SAKICHI TOYODA

Throughout my career as chief learning officer in multiple companies, I have been intrigued by people, how they behave, how they learn and grow, and how they manage themselves and others.

Some people are inquisitive all the time and seem to have retained their original childhood curiosity. Others are struggling to show up curiously, as they are burdened by stress or have lost some of their curiosity along the way. I ended up calling the curious colleagues "A-players" and their more incurious colleagues "B-players." I have spent many years observing the characteristics of A-players. I have also reflected on how to influence B-players toward more inquisitive behavior.

A-players are fearless. They have an infectious curiosity about them. They are interested in the world, in others, and in themselves. They can be described as having confident humility. They know they do not know everything yet are confident enough to tell others they are ignorant about many things. They are hungry, though, to learn and fix their lack of knowledge through incessant questioning, above-average interest, reading, and other exploratory means of knowledge acquisition.

The best employees are A-players. They are hungry for information, eager to solve problems, and open to the ideas of colleagues. They have an enhanced ability to learn, ask more unprompted questions, and are not afraid of ambiguous information. They invest time in keeping up to speed with business and colleagues, even when things get tough. If they work for curious bosses and curious organizations, magic happens.

The key insight is they are intentionally curious. They don't leave curiosity to chance. They embrace it proactively and with passion.

Do you know such people? Maybe you are an A-player yourself.

It was only after I learned about the psychology of curiosity that I started calling these colleagues "curious." An A-player's biggest character trait comes down to curiosity. Once I started to understand this, a world opened to me.

I was able to describe curious individuals, how some companies are better at recruiting and keeping them, and how some leaders are thrilled to work with them while others think of them as difficult to manage. It did not take long for me to realize only a minority of our workforce is showing up curiously at work.

I also learned not everybody is an A-player all the time. Depending on the influence of the environment and the frame of mind of the individual, curiosity can grow or lessens. I have seen B-players transform themselves and become A-players. I have experienced companies going to great effort to recruit A-players yet stifled them the moment they walked through the front door. I have also seen A-players become B-players because of things that happened in their lives.

What is interesting is larger entities, such as teams and organizations, can equally behave as A- or B-players.

Let's explore some of the deeper drivers of what makes a curious professional.

CURIOUS PROFESSIONALS GO DEEP AND BROAD

The distinction between narrow and broad curiosity is important when analyzing A-players. Narrow curiosity refers to our interest to learn more about the things we are already familiar with. An example would be an engineer who wants to go deeper and learn more about engineering. Narrow curiosity leads to more specialization as one keeps building on previous knowledge and expertise.

Broad curiosity, on the other hand, focuses on exploring new and previously unknown terrains. Building on our engineering example, here the engineer would want to learn about a new aspect she was not exposed to, such as the customer environment, finance, or anthropology. More than narrow curiosity, broad curiosity requires the person to be extra open to novelty and adopt a continuous learning mindset. It also triggers the individual to be comfortable about being a perpetual novice.

Comparing Narrow and Broad Curiosity

NARROW CURIOSITY	BROAD CURIOSITY
• Leads to specialization • Creates experts • Used for problem solving • Focused on a single expertise • Supports continuous improvement • Extension of exploitation mindset	• Broad vertical transferable skills • Creates generalists • Leads to problem finding • Centered around broad interests • Drives disruptive innovation • Extension of exploration mindset
Useful in predictable environments	Useful in complex systems

I have been mentoring many aspiring professionals who asked me whether to go for a specialist role or a generalist position. My initial advice to them has almost always been to go deep first and establish credibility in one specialization and then expand more broadly. Once they understood the concept, I made sure they appreciated the difference between narrow and broad curiosity through the lens of the environments they found themselves in. Predictable environments value narrow curiosity, complex systems require more broad curiosity.

How would you rate your own environment? Is it predictable or complex? Is there a preference for narrow or broad curiosity given its environmental situation?

Companies such as IBM, Toyota, and others are actively combining both dimensions into what is referred to as the "T-shaped" employee. The vertical bar of the letter T can be regarded as the depth of skills and expertise in a single field of the professional; the horizontal bar is the knowledge of areas other than one's specialization (Thorén 2019).

The power of this model is employees need both. No company is 100 percent predictable or complex. Combining broad and narrow curiosity allows professionals to focus both on deepening their professionalism as well as exploring new terrains. When we spoke, curiosity researcher and leadership consultant Alison Horstmeyer stressed the importance for professionals to be "expert explorers." According to her, "expert explorers" combine the following abilities: listening, asking open-ended questions, having an unselfish attitude, being receptive and open, and reflective behavior.

In most organizations nowadays, broad curiosity leads to progression in terms of upward career movement and faster salary gains, while narrow curiosity in the workplace leads to a certain stagnation, even when it leads to the strengthening of one's individual knowledge.

An interesting dynamic can be observed when considering these two dimensions. Over the last one hundred years, specialization has been preferred over broad curiosity. The narrow is preferred over the whole. This is true in both academics and companies. In medicine, it is not sufficient to be a general neurologist anymore; it is better to be specialized in something specific, such as pain treatment. A consequence is in some environments, being curious can be seen as superficial because of its need for diverse interests rather than focusing on one single skill.

David Epstein in his 2019 book *Range* highlights a similar trend. He explains the twentieth century was all about narrow specialization and wondering more broadly as a generalist was frowned upon. In most teams and organizations, just being the generalist often does not lead to a big bonus or promotion.

Epstein highlights broad curiosity has a positive influence also deepening one's specialization. According to him, narrow curiosity leads to new ideas within the limits of our frame of reference and leads at most to incremental innovation. New knowledge acquired through broad curiosity applied to our own specialization has the potential for bigger innovation as new knowledge can provide a new lens to our known area of expertise. With broad curiosity, you cross over in other areas, providing inspiration to make your own specialization even better (Epstein 2019).

David Epstein shows in his book why narrow curiosity at best leads to narrow improvements, while broad exploration in other territories has the potential for more disruptive innovation (Epstein 2019). Furthermore, the spark new knowledge from unchartered territories can bring has the potential to become a new deep specialization. If you follow this logic, it is possible to become an expert in two (or more) areas. The more areas you become an expert in, the easier it will be to expand your knowledge even further.

When we analyze the recipients of Nobel Prizes over time, we can see a gradual appreciation of broad curiosity is also felt in science. While scientists previously were rewarded for their discoveries in distinct areas, nowadays, scientists who draw new insights by comparing the intersection of two or more areas of expertise (for instance, physics and biology) are more likely to be given this coveted award (Epstein 2019).

In the corporate world, all executives I interviewed for this book were advocating for both specialization and broad exploration. In an increasing number of enterprises, corporate learning and development teams are actively looking for ways to train people beyond the current role and provide space for the employee to learn broadly in a new area of their individual interests. This prepares her for the next role, even if this role is not articulated yet.

PRODUCTIVE VERSUS UNPRODUCTIVE CURIOSITY

Curious professionals use curiosity as a tool to improve things around them.

To allow curiosity in the workplace, it is important to distinguish between productive and unproductive curiosity. A productive curiosity adds value and bolsters organizational performance. An unproductive curiosity is a barrier, as it dilutes organizational focus.

Productive curiosity is curiosity aimed at solving a business problem, at reaching a goal, or at exploring a new horizon. Unproductive curiosity is the type of curiosity with little no or impact. It is the type of curiosity without a clear starting position, focus, and end goal. Unproductive curiosity is like engaging in endless and focus-less team ideation without the subsequent action.

In the private sphere, unproductive curiosity can take the form of binge-watching videos, aimlessly browsing the internet without clear focus or goal. Many of us have experienced the "Internet rabbit hole." We start on a single website, and three hours later, we wake up as if coming out of a dream, still looking at the screen.

Good leaders know when to allow curiosity to be allowed in the team and when to move into action.

Research with leadership teams has shown leaders who are productively curious not only are better than others in exploring new strategies for their organizations, but their curiosity also leads to better operational efficiency. Productive curiosity leads to better question strategies and triggers incremental as well as more disruptive innovation. The same research also uncovered that unproductive curiosity has a higher potential to lead to burnout, while productive curiosity correlates more with happiness at work and at home (Harrison 2021).

THE EXPLORER'S GENE

Many people believe curiosity is an unalterable personality trait. You either have it in abundance or in little supply. This difference shows in our day-to-day actions. Successful entrepreneurs and scientists are especially accredited by others (and often believe so themselves) to possess higher doses of curiosity when compared to others.

Intuitively, this makes sense from observing people around us. We all can observe clear differences in how people show up curiously, in terms of the frequency of its occurrence, the intensity level, the amount of time people are prepared to devote to exploration, and, in general, the openness to and reference for novel experiences. Elon Musk feels like a more curious entrepreneur than you or I are.

One argument says curiosity as a trait could be linked to a specific DNA strand. In the January 2013 *National Geographic* article "Restless Genes," scientist David Dobbs explains 20 percent of human beings have, by birth, a mutated gene, causing them to be more curious and restless. Geneticists believe they have isolated a variant of a gene named "DRD4-7R," which causes people to take more risks in exploring the world, ideas, and people. Mr. Dobbs writes, "Dozens of human studies have found 7R makes people more likely to take risks; explore new places, ideas, foods, relationships, drugs, or sexual opportunities; and generally, embrace movement, change, and adventure. Studies in animals simulating 7R's actions suggest it increases their taste for both movement and novelty." People endowed with this "explorers' gene" would also embrace change and adventure more than others (Gehricke 2015).

The above research would indicate the belief we are born with a fixed amount of curiosity at birth is at least partially plausible. What researchers have found, however, is that belief is at best incomplete.

However, we intuitively know nobody is curious all the time. Next to being endowed at birth with an innate capacity for curiosity, we are equally dependent on our environment for curiosity. Psychologists call this "state curiosity" (Loewenstein 1994). State curiosity indicates our level of curiosity is—at least in part—dependent on the environment and thus constantly in flux.

Depending on the role models we surround ourselves with, the mindset of the direct leader, and the openness culture of our employer and its acceptance of failure, we will fold to the environmental curiosity preference, for better or for worse.

Researchers who have researched twins, particularly in comparing twins reared apart and together, have been able to establish what percentage—on average—is attributable to genetics and what part to nurture. Professor Auke Tellegen from the University of Minnesota and his colleagues have found "on average, about 50 percent of measured personality diversity can be attributed to genetic diversity. The remaining 50 percent is technically classified as all environmental" (Tellegen 1988).

Curiosity is thus both a trait and a state. It is prone to flux. We are in our curiosity zone when things go well, when the individual feels fine, and when the environment is supportive.

There is merit to having the discussion about trait versus state, or rather trait and state. We are all curious in different ways. All children are curious. Many people who do not show curiosity at work end up being extremely curious on weekends when engaging in their hobbies.

State curiosity is, in many ways, more important than trait curiosity. One reason is too much reliance on trait curiosity leads to a fixed mindset where curiosity is an unalterable trait of an individual. Also, it leads to a system of curious haves and have-nots. Intuitively, trait curiosity only makes sense to a certain level. Sure, some people are endowed with more intellectual capacity and more executive decision power than others. Yet at the end of the day, we are all curious about something. I am curious about gardening, scuba-diving, and meditation. You might be interested in very different things.

CURIOSITY AND KNOWLEDGE

Think about a simple, innocent factoid you pick up. Something like the following: people breathe alternatively through one nostril at a time and alternate breathing through the right and left nostrils. Some will dismiss this as being fake news and not give it a second thought, others might be triggered to explore something new they did not know yet about themselves. A third group might already know whether this is true or not.

Let's assume you were not aware of the (in)correct nature of this statement. You did not know you didn't know. It was a non-issue. The moment you read this statement though you took an unconscious decision that determined your subsequent action. Is this a worthwhile enough item to become curious about or shall you disregard it?

Psychologists commonly refer to this phase as "the assessment of novelty potential" (Kashdan 2020). When confronted with something new, people assess the level of novelty by comparing it to your personal values and beliefs (you love to learn new things), previous experience (breathing problems), existing knowledge (having some knowledge about it), your current mindset (tired, hungry, just right, etc.), and a large enough intensity to trigger your interest in the first place.

A second and almost instantaneous decision, which psychologists call "coping potential," is then taken, i.e., an answer to the question "Do I have the skills, expertise, and resources needed to look for a solution? Does knowing or not knowing pose a threat?" (Kashdan 2020). In the above question, knowing how you breathe is not life-threatening, and since you know how to read and have this book as your resource, you have the right tools to find the solution.

If you have answered yes to both novelty potential as well as coping potential, you will experience curiosity. If one of these two would be a no, you will cease to be curious and divert your attention to something else. That's why we are all curious sometimes; only the object and intensity of our curiosity differs. My brother-in-law is hugely interested in car mechanics, while I could not be bothered about it.

Researchers have been able to plot the relationship between curiosity and knowledge as an inverted U-shape in a graph (Loewenstein 1994).

THE RELATIONSHIP BETWEEN CURIOSITY AND KNOWLEDGE

When is curiosity is at its peak?
when our knowledge of something or someone is high enough to awaken our interest

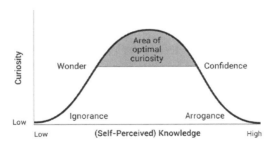

* adapted from George Loewenstein

THE AREA OF IGNORANCE: UNKNOWN UNKNOWNS

As we can conclude from the above example, I cannot be curious about "unknown unknowns." If I have no knowledge about something, I cannot be curious. Once I hear there is something like "alternate nostril breathing," I might decide to move upward on the graph and start wondering whether this is true (or not). On the graph, my curiosity appetite is close to zero when I have no knowledge about something. Otherwise put: if we are unconsciously incompetent, we will not take steps to start exploring, discovering, or learning.

Take, for instance, the concept of machine learning. If you are, like me, not a computer expert, you might have heard of the term, you might have some vague notion of what it means. If you have never heard of the term, you will not have it on your intellectual radar and thus not be curious about it. Since I mentioned machine learning, you just might become a tad curious and do a quick search on the internet.

Depending on your personal internet exploration strategy, you might check out Wikipedia, YouTube, or just see what links Google throws up on your screen. If you are more than a bit curious, you might even want to check out the free Stanford University machine learning course on Coursera (https://www.coursera.org/learn/machine-learning). You have become consciously aware of your incompetence and are moving toward becoming consciously competent, albeit mildly in this case.

This is how curiosity works. Curiosity builds on knowledge and knowledge builds on curiosity. We need curiosity to get started with learning and the more we learn and the more knowledge we acquire, the more curious we become. The curve starts going up. The more we know, the more we are motivated to learn more. After the Coursera course, you might think about reading a book out of curiosity, take another course, or see whether you can code some machine learning algorithm yourself.

When reading about "unknown unknowns," one might remember the famous words by US Secretary of Defense Donald Rumsfeld during a press meeting in February 2002. When confronted by journalists about lack of evidence linking Iraq to terrorist organizations and whether Saddam Hussein, the leader of Iraq, was supplying arms of mass destruction to rogue organizations, Mr. Rumsfeld responded cryptically:

"Reports that say something hasn't happened are always interesting to me, because as we know, there are known knowns; there are things we know we know. We also know there are known unknowns; that is to say we know there are some things we do not know. But there are also unknown unknowns—the ones we don't know we don't know" (Rumsfeld 2002).

Journalists were baffled by his answer and were left guessing whether Iraq and Saddam Hussein had, in fact, relationships with terrorist groups. What this statement did do was win Mr. Rumsfeld the 2003 Foot in Mouth Award for the most baffling comment by a public figure (Livio 2017).

THE OPTIMAL AREA OF CURIOSITY: WONDER

The sweet spot for curiosity is between the stages of wonder and confidence on the graph. In his 2005 Stanford commencement address, Steve Jobs explained this curiosity space well when he terminated his speech with "Stay hungry, stay foolish." Earlier in his talk, he had already alluded to this phrase when he said the following words to the Stanford students:

> Your time is limited, so don't waste it living someone else's life. Don't be trapped by dogma—which is living with the results of other people's thinking. Don't let the noise of others' opinions drown out your own inner voice. And most important, have the courage to follow your heart and intuition. They somehow already know what you truly want to become. Everything else is secondary.

> —Steve Jobs

We are most curious when we already have knowledge about something. If I already know 180 capitals of the 195 or so countries in the world, I will be more motivated to learn the remaining 15 than when I barely know a handful of them. The more knowledge you have, the more you will be curious.

THE AREA OF DECLINE: OVERCONFIDENCE

You will notice the right side of the graph shows a dip. If knowledge about something (or someone) is perceived to be high, arrogance sets in, and curiosity drops. It is not when we know a lot we lose curiosity, it is when we think we know it all that we stop learning or exploring.

Let's continue our machine learning example. If you happen to be a computer specialist who has worked in machine learning for many years and think you have reached your top, then you might stop learning new insights. During your work, you rely on your experience and routines you learned before. Gradually, your knowledge will erode. Hopefully, you will rekindle your knowledge or otherwise turn your intellectual curiosity to some new area to explore. The most curious people like to be intellectual omnivores. Ditto for companies.

I highlighted earlier that overconfidence and arrogance are barriers to curiosity. Research by Yusuke Tsugawa, assistant professor of medicine at UCLA, shows experienced medical doctors are less successful in diagnosing patients when compared to their younger—and less experienced—colleagues (Tsugawa 2017).

Counterintuitive as it is, younger doctors with fewer years of experience are better at diagnosing patients. This is true for two reasons: the first one has to do with curiosity, the other with access to knowledge. Young doctors know they have a solid grounding of knowledge and are comfortable with having most of the knowledge for a good diagnosis cognitively readily available. At the same time, these young doctors are acutely aware they lack experience and/or certain knowledge, compelling them to discuss with colleagues and look up extra information before they cast a diagnosis upon their patients.

The other reason is one about access to knowledge: young doctors have had access to more up-to-date knowledge during their studies and treat more patients in their residency years than their older peers.

THE DUNNING-KRUGER EFFECT

I alluded already to this dimension. It is not actual, but perceived knowledge that leads to arrogance. In psychology, two researchers, David Dunning and Justin Kruger, discovered a type of cognitive bias in which people believe they are smarter and more capable than they really are (Kruger 1999).

We all think we are better parents than the neighbors, better professionals than our peers, and deserve the year-end bonus more than others. This is true for pretty much all people. Executive coach and business writer Marshall Goldsmith mentioned over 90 percent of drivers think they're above average behind the wheel of a car. Ditto with salespeople: even average salespeople think of themselves better at closing deals than others. If they cannot close a deal, they claim it is because of external factors affecting the deal, not because of their skills (Goldsmith 2007).

In their 1999 study, what David Dunning and Justin Kruger found is we overestimate our competence and underestimate the competence of others. We think of ourselves as more knowledgeable and at the same time think of others as being less able. After taking the online Coursera machine learning course, I might suddenly become overconfident about my machine learning knowledge. I might start thinking about talking confidently about machine learning at a dinner party because I assume I know more than others about it.

How do you know you are showing up curiously? Mike Pino, partner at PwC, shared with me his strategy for determining whether he is performing in his zone of curiosity. According to him, he knows he is in the right curious frame of mind when he can reflect on his self-narratives. He regularly assesses himself to see whether he finds himself in the right zone or whether he finds himself in an unconscious incurious mental spiral. At that moment, he redirects his thoughts to look at things differently. This invariably brings new insights, new information, and new experiences to the foreground.

Only with self-awareness is one able to read one's own competence and capabilities objectively. The challenge is: self-awareness is often in low supply. Think of the potential danger of the Dunning-Kruger effect for people in power making important decisions in the workplace. Power, whether it is in the hands of managers or experts, can have a blinding effect and can make us overconfident in our capabilities, disregard the advice given by team members, and become incurious to alternatives.

To put you out of your misery about the nostril breathing question: Normal humans breathe through one nostril at the time, and we alternate every forty minutes or so between nostrils. This has been known for ages in the Indian Yogic traditions. I was introduced to this when I lived in Bangalore, India, when I got exposed to the practice of yoga and meditation.

After observing all these benefits, I have been asking myself, why is it then that many companies are stifling the curiosity of their employees the moment they join? Why is it, leaders say they value curiosity, yet prefer to manage B-players, thinking A-players are unruly, difficult to manage, and distract the team from its efficiency focus?

Business professors Andy Boynton and Bill Fisher describe this underlying challenge at the start of their book *Virtuoso Teams* eloquently:

> It started quite a few years ago with the disturbing recognition that each month we'd work with yet another organization dedicated to attracting "great" people into its workforce, to become the "employer of choice" in their field, to be seen as a talent magnet on the university campuses where they recruited at, and yet, year after year, despite the continuous addition of constantly "great" people, these same firms would return, unfailingly, average results (Boynton 2005).

To answer these questions, we need to dig into the psyche of managerial thinking of last century. We will do this in the next chapter. We will also enter a dialogue about why curiosity is needed now more than ever and why curious employees need curious environments to thrive.

The Big Ideas

The landscape of curiosity is becoming clearer. A-players are claiming their rightful position in the world of business. They make faster careers, and they often make more money as a result. They tend to be more engaged, more productive, and readier to embrace the change and transformation agendas of their employers. They are hungrier for knowledge and learn faster than others. This is because they are more intentional about their curiosity.

Curious professionals go deep and wide. They combine narrow and broad curiosity to their benefit. They are deploying productive curiosity to their benefit, allowing them to be more effective in the present as well as being open to new opportunities.

Curiosity follows an inverted U-shape. When we don't know that we don't know, we cannot be curious. When we think we know a lot about something or someone, our curiosity sees a decline, and we stop exploring. The ideal zone of curiosity is when we have some knowledge yet are eager to learn more. Automatically following from this is that curiosity needs knowledge to build on, and the more knowledge we have, the more questions we can ask and inferences we can make.

Questions for Reflection

- What percentage of the new information and learning you explore is in your area of expertise, and what percentage is about exploring previously unknown terrains?

- In your present job, where do you/your peers/ your manager/your company find yourself on the inverted U-shape: at the level of ignorance, wonder, or arrogance?

- Look for an area of your life where you are not in the zone of curiosity. What can you do to find yourself in that zone?

- What definition does curiosity have in your workplace: is it seen as a productive or unproductive activity?

- Is curiosity—the productive type—encouraged for all levels of employees in your organization, or only for specific groups?

3

WHY CURIOSITY, WHY NOW?

"Curiosity is critical for success in our increasingly complex world."
—VASANT NARASIMHAN, CEO OF NOVARTIS INTERNATIONAL

Who remembers "Kodak moments?" All those moments worthy of picture taking, a visual reminder of something meaningful in our lives. Who remembers when we had a specialized device for taking pictures? A time when we did not have smartphones doubling as a camera?

Until approximately twenty years ago, there was a delay between taking a picture and seeing it printed on paper. It could take a couple of days or several weeks. It all depended on how quickly you finished your roll of twenty-four or thirty-six pictures before you took it to the store to be developed.

In those days, one had the choice between three brands: the US company Kodak, the Japanese company Fujifilm, and the smaller Belgian company Agfa-Gevaert. I lived in the People's Republic of China in the early 1990s and traveled the country extensively. I still remember the three colors these companies represented in the tourist selling booths. Kodak came in a yellow box, Fujitsu in a green one, and Agfa came in orange.

What would Kodak's creator, George Eastman, do today if he learned the iconic company known to every single woman and man globally, the company he had built from scratch, eventually went bankrupt and was largely forgotten? He had revolutionized his industry and had given joy to so many people. As early as the year 1900, his "Brownie" had given kids a new toy they could capture the world with. Yet all this magic eroded over time and was lost (Eastman 2015).

The management for generations coming after him shed his entrepreneurial spirit and became closed-minded, arrogant, and intent on avoiding risk. They used the past as the single tool to predict the future and valued like-minded people over diversity. They stopped exploring. Deep down, they pay lip service to innovation, even when they were the inventors of next generation digital products.

Companies come and go. Especially the companies that stop being intentional about exploration and curiosity. They stop being relevant and are overtaken by companies not afraid of exploring the new.

THE WORLD AS WE KNOW IS CHANGING

Companies cannot afford to be incurious. An organization that is not curious will become complacent, will not learn from mistakes, will be arrogant and will miss the corner of innovation in the light of new competition.

Recent fundamental forces are encouraging leaders to rethink their status quo radically. We are experiencing a rise in social tension, economic nationalization, technological revolution, and the importance of global health (Bhattacharya 2020).

- Technology has been a disrupter for the last thirty years. The internet of things, machine learning, artificial intelligence, and increased computing power have reshaped the way we do business. The era of computer and automation is making place for an era of cyber connectedness of physical systems.

- Societal changes have influenced our collective management thinking. We see a rise in nationalization and protectionism across countries, making it harder to run global operations. Think of Brexit and the US government limiting entry visas. COVID-19 has shown the world is a vulnerable place. Only by concerted effort and solidarity with each other can we face global health challenges. The planet is also finally becoming an important board agenda. Voices all around the world have been advocating for societies, corporations, and individuals to start focusing on the need to preserve the planet for the next generations.

- Economic disruption: In the light of accelerated economic activity toward the fourth industrial revolution spearheaded by infotech and biotech, virtually every industry is being transformed and is seeing new entrants entering their markets. No single industry is spared from an increased pace of disruption, speed, and new entrants.

- Workforce transformation: Many countries see an increase in the gig economy, a labor market characterized by the prevalence of short-term contracts or freelance work as opposed to permanent jobs. Mervi Koivisto, a successful Finnish entrepreneur, told me the majority of the best university students in her country set up their own companies straight out of school rather than apply for a job. Additionally, after the long work-from-home period during COVID-19, employees are demanding a new mental contract with their employers or are leaving the company altogether.

Companies turn over at a more accelerated rate than before. Management Professor Stephane Garelli from the Swiss-based business school IMD shares in the 1950s, big companies used to have a lifespan of sixty-one years. Now it is down to eighteen (Garelli 2016).

Why is it so hard for leaders to adapt? One reason for this decline is the environment has become less predictable; another reason is companies have been replicating the mental models of the stable twentieth century to run companies in the volatile twenty-first century. This includes our mental model about how to make the best use of people.

REWRITING THE RULES AT SPEED

When talking to Simon Brown, chief learning officer at Novartis, he shared a simple comparison. In a 2018 survey about the innovation appetite of companies with chief information officers, only 1 percent of them indicated they were interested in blockchain. Fast forward two years to 2020, and the company LinkedIn with their yearly learning survey report listed blockchain as the hottest technology skill to acquire.

A new playbook for leaders is being written. Changes surrounding us at a meta-level are big.

COVID-19 shook the world. It has given impetus to a global deconditioning of our deeply ingrained beliefs about how we should live our lives, treat our employees, and manage our organizations. They—professionals of all levels—have become used to the advantages of working from home.

The fact so many companies are so vocal about allowing employees to decide for themselves where they want to work tells a deeper story. Employees are emancipating and are refusing to simply go with the flow their organizations dictate. They have ideas of their own, not only of how they want to live their lives, but also ideas that could lead to new products and services for their companies. The curious employee has arisen. Curious individuals want to create their environment and actively build the future alongside others.

Leaders are trying to balance the solid old and the liquid new. In many industries, lowest cost is replaced by highest speed, resulting in leaders rethinking their global production footprint. Leaders are gradually realizing efficiency and operational excellence are only one side of the coin. The other side requires resilience, openness, and curiosity.

Broader than individuals and organizations, an incurious society will see its decline. History has numerous examples of societies that became complacent and subsequently disappeared altogether.

Curiosity is a key ingredient to build entirely new foundations for our economic and social systems. If we fail to do this, crises will deepen and leave the world even less sustainable, less equal, and more fragile. During the COVID-19 crisis, companies, universities, and others joined forces to develop diagnostics, therapeutics, and possible vaccines, establishing testing centers, creating mechanisms for tracing infections, and delivering telemedicine.

Imagine what could be possible if similar concerted efforts were made in every sector.

RETHINKING MENTAL MODELS

We have been carrying with us the legacy of the twentieth century. That legacy made us who we are today, how we view the world, how we interact with each other, and how we manage ourselves, our environments, and our organizations. Most of the time, we don't even know why we do the things we do, as often we do them unconsciously or they were passed down by previous generations. A fish does not know it swims in water.

Our mental models we have built in the twentieth century are up for renewal. Where the old model was built on an industrial standard of stable and steady exploitation, the current model requires empowerment, agility, autonomy, and exploration. In a nutshell: curiosity. For this, we need curious professionals, leaders, teams, and organizations.

While some have been embracing curiosity, most have been undervaluing and under-focusing on curiosity as a force for good. As I mentioned in the introduction, Harvard researcher Francesca Gino found though most leaders say they value curiosity, they actually stifle it (Gino 2018). We will expand on this in the leadership chapter.

While the twentieth century was the century of industrial conglomerates, the twenty-first century is the century of ideas. It took Marriott International eighty-eight years to amass enough hotel properties to boast 690 thousand rooms in eighty countries. It took Airbnb only four years to reach 650 thousand rooms in 197 countries. In early 2022, the market capitalizations of Marriott and Airbnb were respectively 54 billion dollars and 104 billion dollars.

The twenty-first century has shown us the world is not the stable predictable space we thought it was. Every human being was affected by the COVID-19 pandemic. The essayist and mathematical statistician Nassim Nicholas Taleb has coined a phrase for such an event: a black swan event. A black swan event is an unpredictable or unforeseen event, typically one with extreme consequences (Taleb 2007).

Not a single industry has avoided radical changes in recent history. The recent COVID-19 crisis has added an unpredictability factor. We are more fragile than we previously thought. In times of change, the certainties of the past are a bad guide toward the future.

The COVID-19 pandemic was not the only event to herald a new era. We have been experiencing an acceleration of our daily environment and our industrial landscapes for more than a generation. Stability was not a strong part of our equation over the last twenty or so years.

Scholars agree on is systems in stability don't require much innovation. In stability, systems try as much as possible to maintain the status quo. They overvalue exploitation and undervalue exploration. Once at cruising speed, individuals and organizations focused on exploitation emphasize old certainties and try to achieve continuity through stability. The dominant mindset is to stay focused on old certainties and create value through efficiency and effectiveness. The preferred strategy tools for corporations are planning and control cycles.

In times of distress, however, the downside of an exploitation-driven mindset becomes obvious: stability leads to stagnation. Though it might feel comfortable in the short term, it hides a long-term evil highlighted well by Herbert Gerjuoy, as quoted by the futurist Alvin Toffler in *Future Shock* in 1970:

"The illiterate of the twenty-first century will not
be those who cannot read and write, but those
who cannot learn, unlearn, and relearn."

The same goes for the incurious of the twenty-first century.

Are we suffering from anosognosia, a neurological condition where the patient is unaware of their neurological deficit or psychiatric condition? Many companies and individuals are sleepwalking in plain daylight, not knowing when competition will hit them or when their skills will not be relevant anymore. They have relied on their automatic pilot and perpetuated the past rather than reinvented the future.

This is what happened to Kodak, Nokia, Blockbuster, and many other companies we will describe who have shown what it is to be incurious. This is also the fate of those incurious individuals who don't invest in their skills, network, and themselves.

The main point I am making is something scholars also agree on. Curiosity is more important than previously thought for the productivity, innovation, and overall well-being of individuals, teams, and organizations. What we know from the field of positive psychology is the curiosity levels of individuals and companies are not fixed but can be developed. Indeed, with the right focus and intention, organizations can tweak their culture, processes, and practices in favor of balancing execution and innovation, exploitation and exploration.

CHARLIE CHAPLIN

Corporations nowadays are grappling with an important dilemma. Do we need to continue to scale a profitable past, explore an unknown and uncertain future, or do both?

I don't think there is a better metaphor to describe twentieth century management than the one described by Charlie Chaplin in his 1936 film *Modern Times*. In this satirical movie, management is removed from the shop floor, is dressed up at work as if ready for a gala, gives orders through a video screen, and has time to read the newspaper leisurely. Management is only interested in increasing efficiency and maximizing production, even if this means cutting lunch all together and decreasing the wellness of the workers on the shop floor even more.

Workers, on the other hand, are presented as mindless cogs in a perpetual system. Worse even: when they think for themselves, the production line hampers. Workers must punch the clock if they go to the bathroom, and they are even checked up on in the privacy of the bathroom. If they stay too long, the manager appears on a video screen pushing them to go to work. Charlie Chaplin's persona experiences a nervous breakdown after having been too long in the belly of such an industrial machine.

We might laugh at the comic representation of modern times in Chaplin's movie. The underlying mental model is sadly still being practiced today in many organizations around the world. It clearly sounds like the working conditions inside the present-day Amazon warehouses.

It goes further—the use of fear to manage people; the dichotomy between workers and management, the doers, and thinkers where the doers are not supposed to do any thinking (and equally managers are not incentivized to roll up their sleeves), and a bigger focus on efficiency than on employee wellness. Sure, we have modernized quite a number of practices, yet high levels of burnout our employees are experiencing are masking a deeper challenge faced by corporations. The environment might have changed, but the old managerial mindset has remained.

We have collectively learned from mistakes and have improved in many ways. Deep down, however, in the belly of our unconscious managerial mindsets, things have not changed dramatically in the way we think about efficiency and manage our employees; the way we reward, promote, and recognize them. Or the way we approach innovation. We are risk averse and react negatively to errors of our employees. We are also more comfortable with maintaining the status quo over exploring new paths.

Instilling fear in the workforce might work in industrial environments where processes are straightforward and immutable, where the employee will only encounter predictable problems solved by preconfigured solutions, and where the employee is not required to come up with improvement ideas.

The knowledge-worker's day is different. She needs to do complex problem-solving and even engage in problem-finding before a problem has arisen. No employee manual can list every possible answer to every single problem. Instead of being cut off from decision making and removed from the creativity and innovation loop, knowledge workers need to possess decision-making authority where the action is. Companies are rapidly replacing repetitive, low-impact jobs with technology and need knowledge workers for their ideas and creativity.

I believe companies have two choices. The first one is to stick our proverbial heads in the ground and continue the path we know best, perpetuating the past. The second one is to be openminded to whatever the future has in store for us and be flexible, humble, and adaptive.

TRAITS OF INCURIOUS COMPANIES

Kodak did not fail because of technology but because it had lost its curiosity muscle. It stopped asking and allowing questions or being humble in the light of changes. It focused on exploitation at the expense of exploration. Their prevailing organizational culture in the 1990s was one of self-righteousness, arrogance, complacency, lacking any sense of urgency to embrace novelty, and focusing on continuing the past rather than preparing for the future. The management in the company was driven by cozy golden hand-cuffs and incentives, encouraging keeping the status quo rather than challenging it. While they were the inventors of the digital camera technology, they failed miserably in commercializing it globally, promptly heralding the company's own demise.

Even the innovations they initiated were grounded in their old business paradigms; they innovated only by tweaking their known strategies and business models. They remained within a familiar mindset and did not change the underlying culture. The company was also highly hierarchical and did not let ideas flow across levels sufficiently.

In an interview with Prof. Dr. Nick van Dam, ex-chief learning officer of McKinsey & Company and now human development scientist at IE University in Spain, shared a personal observation from the time he had visited Kodak's campus:

> Each management level on the Kodak campus in Rochester had their own restaurant reserved only for their level. Meeting with people from different levels and exchanging ideas in an informal setting was thus impeded. The company lacked organizational agility and failed to reinvent itself beyond their known world.

It was not that the company did not see the decline in analog film on the horizon. After all, the company had attracted the best brains in the market, had access to global information, and had a stellar strategy team and smart people filling all ranks of the company. Something else was at play.

I call this "collective stupidity." I have seen it in other companies: Kodak's collective intelligence had become less than the sum of the individual intelligence of all its people. In other words, they had become an incurious company. Their collective mindset had led them astray.

When considering a case like Kodak, probably other examples come to mind of companies that missed a crucial pivot in history. Some examples:

- The US-based company Blockbuster was a big player in the videocassette rental business before online movie channels started. They turned down a proposal by Netflix to join forces and jointly create a new de facto standard for renting and viewing films.

- General Motors explored the potential of electric cars yet decided to discontinue developments in this area in 2003. That same year, an individual who had no prior experience in the car business started his electric car business. Elon Musk launched Tesla.

- In the late 1990s, the Finnish company Nokia was on top of the mobile telephone world. Around the world, their products were so popular, the Nokia name became the adopted word to describe any mobile phone. Nokia had taken other companies like Ericsson, Alcatel, Lucent, and other traditional telephone companies by surprise in the early 1990s. Like these companies before them, Nokia's management was so focused on efficiency and building on their past successes they stopped listening for new clues. New entrants in their market were sensing phones were less about voice, and more about pocket computers.

These companies were very successful, had great brands, and were attracting the best talent, yet they were not able to capitalize on their success over time. What was the root cause that led to their demise? It was their mental model of the way companies were supposed to function. I call such companies incurious companies. They lacked openness to face present and future challenges.

Such companies display the following characteristics:

- Collective cognitive bias: focus on like-mindedness and groupthink. Low on diversity and cognitive flexibility.

- Disregard for an evolving environment and new entrants, focus on what has worked in the past, and a low sense of urgency and difficulty to embrace change.

- Focus on the known world, a mindset of confirmation bias, and no proactive exploration of new territories.

- Adherence to efficiency strategy based on historic expertise: the past is the only guide to predict the future, and processes are designed to keep status quo.

- Managerial arrogance: management is placed on a pedestal. Past individual success of executives and the overall success of the organization leads to a feeling of invulnerability and aggressive behavior. Management does the thinking, the rest of the organization is considered as implementation power, not as a source of ideas. In such systems, the level of managerial humility is low.

- Prevailing efficiency objectives at the expense of effectiveness: preference for implementation is more important than ideation, exploitation of the status quo is more important than exploration of the future.

- A belief that curiosity is distracting from their efficiency focus and, at best, marginally linked to continuous improvement.

In my work with companies, I have noticed it is always possible to come up with reasons why the companies we work for are to be considered curious. This is always hopeful. Every company has positive elements in its culture to build on. At the same time, what is more important is to look beyond the obvious and dig deeper. What we say or believe might not fully reflect reality.

In 2019, 184 CEOs of large organizations released a statement on the new purpose of an organization. In this statement, they pleaded, the purpose of the organization was not to solely focus on shareholders, but instead to embrace all stakeholders: customers, employees, suppliers, community members, and shareholders (Business Roundtable 2019).

One would imagine, at least for these 184 companies, active steps would have been taken to move the needle in support of these five stakeholders. Lucian Bebchuk and Roberto Tallarita of Harvard Law School have, however, not found evidence to this effect. They argue unless CEO incentives and local legislation changes, the reality on the ground will not change, even if CEOs make overt commitments (Bebchuk 2020).

Those companies who adopt a balance between genuine exploration and exploitation outmaneuver those companies who maintain an exploitation-only paradigm. The emphasis in a curious organization is not on old certainties, but on new possibilities. Instead of focusing solely on getting results through stable, efficient, and effective processes, these companies focus on renewal, building potential, and adopting rejuvenation and innovation processes. The dominant mindset is then one of open-minded, confident humility, where the main role of leadership is not so much on providing clarity, but on orchestrating new opportunities.

With the advent of artificial intelligence technologies, computers will be replacing highly repetitive jobs and highly analytical ones. Humans will be focusing on those jobs requiring meaning, creativity, and agile inference making across domains and complex problem-finding. They need safe spaces to explore.

Before we plunge into workplace curiosity, I suggest we charge ourselves at one more stop. To become better at curiosity, we need to understand what the underlying psychology of curiosity is. We will see, while curiosity is powerful, it is also fragile and multifaceted. It is also highly dependent on the way people and organizations are tolerant of stress. This is the topic of the next chapter.

If you have taken your individual curiosity diagnostic, or intend to, we will also provide an insight in the three applications of curiosity: intellectual, empathic, and intrapersonal curiosity. In the next chapter, I let you know how you can take this diagnostic. First, I suggest you take a moment to reflect on the big ideas of this chapter as well as the reflection questions.

The Big Ideas

A new wind is blowing in these early years of the twenty-first century. While the twentieth century was one of large industrial concerns, the twenty-first century is the century of ideas. Times are changing and they are changing fast. There are undeniable indications the solutions of the past that got us to where we are now will not carry us forward very long in the future.

The risk avoidance controls put in place need to be finally pulled back. It is time to start balancing exploitation with exploration. It is time for organizations and their leadership teams to become curious.

We need new ideas, new questions, and new answers. We also need to foster environments that create the right conditions and cultures for employees to show up curiously. We don't have to start from scratch as many companies have shown the way.

Once we are aware of the deeper drivers of historic context of why we managed organizations and people the way we do, we can start looking at the world with new eyes and make changes.

Questions for Reflection

- What is your enterprise doing well to allow for curiosity? What could be done better?

- Is curiosity celebrated at work?

- Would you say you/your company are/is better prepared for the next ten to twenty years?

- What is your own strategy to counter a conformist mindset on a daily basis? How open are you to ideas that go against your own thinking?

- What would you advise your management team or board to change first?

4

THE PSYCHOLOGY
OF CURIOSITY

———

"Human beings, by changing the inner attitudes of their minds, can change the outer aspects of their life."

—WILLIAM JAMES, PHILOSOPHER,
HISTORIAN, AND PSYCHOLOGIST

If one wants to encourage more curiosity in a workplace, it's helpful to understand how it works in our brains.

How is it possible some people are more curious than others? What is it? Is it indeed a mono-dimensional trait we can turn on or off? We have explored some of this together in earlier chapters. In this chapter, we will be deepening this understanding and explore more. We will discuss what the biggest barrier to curiosity is. We will further discuss how we can make curiosity tangible and what are the three practical applications needed to understand curiosity so we can action it.

WHAT THE RESEARCH TELLS US

I hope you are warming up to the notion that once we open the lid of curiosity, its underlying reality is a bit more complex than what we previously thought it would be, yet exciting, nonetheless. As we will see, there is still much we don't know, yet some areas we are certain about.

The research on curiosity started as late as the 1950s by the seminal work of the Canadian psychologist Daniel Berlyne. He established much of the groundwork upon which all subsequent study of curiosity has still largely been based. He was one of the first ones to recognize and describe the multifaceted psychological nature of curiosity. He consolidated curiosity into four aspects.

1. **Perceptual Curiosity**: Dr. Berlyne describes perceptual curiosity as a "drive which is aroused by novel stimuli and reduced by continued exposure to these stimuli" (Berlyne 1954). This type of curiosity describes the exploratory behavior of infants and adults, as well as animals. It gets triggered by sensory stimuli. We hear a knock on the door, and we look up. We see a headline in the newspaper, triggering us to read more, etc. As soon as the intensity of the stimulus has subsided, we lose interest and focus on other things. Perceptual curiosity is less often experienced in a knowledge intensive workplace, apart from jobs high on sensory input such as advertisement, cuisine, arts, and crafts.

2. **Epistemic Curiosity**: This type of curiosity can be defined as "the appetite, desire, and thirst for knowledge" (Berlyne 1954). Contrary to perceptual curiosity,

fading once we have become familiar with the object of our interest, epistemic curiosity increases with exposure. The more we become familiar with a topic of intellectual pursuit, the more we want to learn. For some of us, this pursuit can take a lifetime. Another difference is epistemic curiosity is purely cognitive and does not require a sensory trigger. While perceptual curiosity can be found also in animals, epistemic curiosity is practiced solely by humans. Applications can be a scientist like Albert Einstein exploring the universe or an individual reading an informative book about curiosity. By its nature, epistemic curiosity is associated with learning and triggers memory and recall.

3. **Specific Curiosity**: Specific curiosity refers to the "desire for a particular piece of information" as epitomized by the attempt to solve a puzzle, to find the answer to a trivia question, to recall the name of the actor who starred in a movie, etc. (Loewenstein 1994).

4. **Diversive Curiosity**: The object of diversive curiosity is broad-based and non-specific. It refers to curiosity about transient or superficial issues. It is often related to impulsive behavior and a sense of boredom (Lievens 2022).

A combination of perceptual/epistemic and specific/diversive is also possible. For instance,

- perceptual/specific: looking up because of a single knock on a door, observing a new colleague entering the room

- perceptual/diversive: scanning the horizon, scanning emails, reading newspaper headlines; for animals: a rat exploring a maze

- epistemic/specific: the desire to solve a problem or scientific inquiry and exploring something specific in depth, such as reading an unknown theory or solving a specific customer challenge

- epistemic/diversive: flipping television channels with a remote control to counter boredom, killing time with internet or unfocused social media browsing

Building on the work of Berlyne and others, current researchers have continued to solve the riddle of curiosity. One of my favorite models is espoused by researcher Todd Kashdan. He and his colleagues have distilled five different distinct dimensions of curiosity. You will recognize some overlap with the earlier work of Berlyne, yet they go beyond the concepts of the old master (Kashdan 2020).

1. **Joyous Exploration**: This is the archetype of curiosity in most cultures. It is about the joy we derive from exploring something new in the world around us. Joyous exploration is the playful curiosity kids or young animals have when attempting to make sense of the world. For adults, it is the spark driving us to proactively seek knowledge and information in the pursuit of learning and growth. Most hobbies are a good example of this type of curiosity.

2. **Deprivation Sensitivity**: This refers to the type of curiosity coming from an anxious feeling of not knowing

or having an answer. It can be simply the feeling of not knowing where you left your car keys, the worry in waiting for a medical report or school results, or when we encounter a disturbing problem at work. The George Orwell example of the clock striking thirteen in the first chapter is an example of this type of curiosity. The better we are at this type of curiosity, the easier we can deal with problems at hand. We are more productive at finding solutions to bridge our knowledge gap and solve the problem.

3. **Stress Tolerance**: The relationship between curiosity and stress is an inverse one. When we are stressed, we lose our capacity to be curious. Stress tolerance is about resilience and the ability to fight stress, doubts, confusion, and uncertainties when faced with something new. The higher our personal tolerance for stress, the easier we are at embracing change, new situations, and people. The lower it is, the more we are prone to paralysis when facing novelty.

4. **Social Curiosity**: This is the realm of interpersonal curiosity. Social curiosity dimension refers to our interest in wanting to know what other people are thinking and doing. It is the level of openness we have toward others, their thoughts, and their feelings. It measures how much we are interested in how other people think, feel, and behave, and how deeply we can relate to them and put ourselves in other people's shoes.

5. **Risk Taking**: This dimension refers to our willingness to take risks in the pursuit of acquiring varied, complex,

and often intense experiences. Think about wanting to drive fast cars, gamble, and take business risks.

In the sphere of work, apart from "risk taking," all these dimensions are important aspects for productive curiosity to occur. Note that these dimensions are not cumulative. It is possible for somebody to be high on joyous exploration and low on deprivation sensitivity or be high on social curiosity and low on the other dimensions (Kashdan 2020).

STRESS: ONE OF THE BIGGEST BARRIERS TO CURIOSITY

As mentioned, there exists an inverse relationship between curiosity and stress. The more we are stressed because of workload, interpersonal tensions in the workplace, or because of internal drivers, the harder it is for us to face the unknown.

In a three-hundred-thousand-people-strong global company where I served as chief learning officer, consumption of employees' learning fell by 50 percent in the first couple of weeks after the first COVID-19 lockdown started.

This is a normal reaction: in the face of change or stress, people first focus on survival, on the present. Only when they find they can deal with the new situation, can they decide whether they are fine to focus again on their future growth and development.

Stress has the effect of inviting tunnel vision as one's openness to alternatives gets shut off. This does not have to happen only in extreme situations. Normal everyday workplace situations can also prevent individuals from being curious. This origin of stress can originate from within the employee, such as internal individual psychological states, fear of not being good enough, fear of not being seen as a team player or being seen as loyal, or fear of being singled out. Stress is expressed in the following terms: "I am not good enough," "What would people think of me?"

Curiosity requires a level of vulnerability, because if you try and fail, your vulnerability is exposed.

Learning innovator Clark Quinn has been reflecting intensively on this topic. He shared with me: "A major reason why our curiosity is weakened is our brains are constantly seeking prediction, confirmation of our patterns and beliefs." According to him, curiosity is the sensation of surprise when something does not correspond to our view of the world.

> Our curious or incurious reaction is driven by either freeze, flight, or fight. Freeze is a reaction to a stimulus that is too strong. We act with paralysis. Flight, on the other hand, is when we actively push away the object of curiosity (e.g., when we don't raise a question out of fear of being seen as stupid). Lastly, a fighting response is a more positive alternative when we face the novelty head-on and start to explore the exciting uncertainty.

In short: a little bit of stress is good and helps curiosity. You have heightened levels of curiosity when you go for an interview or start your first day at work. Too much anxiety, however, leads to paralysis and our curiosity will be stifled at that moment.

Amy Edmondson describes eloquently in her 2018 book *The Fearless Organization* that psychologically low safety environments are especially prone to inviting reductive behavior (Edmondson 2018). In a 2017 study of Canadian workers by SurveyMonkey, six in ten see "barriers to asking questions" where they work (SurveyMonkey 2020). A feeling of safety enhances our exploration mindset or prevents it.

Stress tolerance has an influence on all other dimensions. If one's tolerance for stress is low, it will affect curiosity in the other dimensions negatively. If indeed stress is high because of an intrinsic driver (e.g., fear of not fitting in) or external drivers (e.g., too high workload and not time to reflect or explore), then people will show up less curiously at work.

It is, therefore, important for employers to make employees self-aware through training of their intrinsic curiosity power of how they can measure their own curiosity level and how they can analyze their individual barriers. Equally, it is important for companies to create the right curiosity conducive culture, processes, and practices to allow curiosity to flourish at work.

If you are interested in exploring the full range of barriers to curiosity, I suggest you read the bonus chapter on "barriers to curiosity," which you can find at: www.globalcuriosityinstitute.com/theworkplacecuriositymanifesto.

THE THREE APPLICATIONS OF CURIOSITY

When looking more closely at curiosity, we can observe three distinct applications: our curiosity about the world, our curiosity about others, and the curiosity we have about ourselves.

I have created a free individual curi[...] an extra aid to help you on your jour[...] riosityinstitute.com/survey. It takes[...] and you will get a personalized curi[...] sent to your email inbox. You don'[...] you do, the information I present in this chapt[...] book might become just a little bit more relevant as you will have clarity about your own curiosity profile.

Allow me to share three distinct applications of curiosity.

INTELLECTUAL CURIOSITY

Intellectual curiosity (curiosity about the world) is the natural interest or drive we have to understand the environment around us. In popular culture, this type of curiosity is often directly associated with curious people. It is characterized in terms of how much joy we get from approaching something new, learning a new language, or embracing change in our organization. This type of curiosity also refers to our drive to solve something we experience as a gap for which we are willing to exert ourselves with proper discipline. Think about Edison exploring several hundred different ways before he found a solution to make his first light bulb. This type of curiosity is sensitive to our level of stress tolerance and the grit we display in the light of challenges.

People who are good at intellectual curiosity are natural explorers, inventors, and travelers. They are driven by either external triggers or simply by their natural thirst for knowledge. They enjoy change and are constantly reinventing themselves. Their

learning is infectious, and they are natural problem
ers. Reading and exploring comes naturally to them.

Leonardo da Vinci, Marie Curie, Walt Disney, Hedy Lamarr,
Katalin Karikó, Elon Musk, Isabella Bird, Richard Branson,
Jack Ma, and many others all personify intellectual curiosity.

Remember what Albert Einstein said:

I don't have any talents; I am only passionately curious.

When people are strong at intellectual curiosity, they are more
likely to seek new information and experiences to make them
think and challenge their assumptions. They have a creative,
restless, and inquiring mind ready to solve a new problem
and learn something new. They thrive when they have a new
intellectual conundrum in front of them. Indeed, they will
likely be good at solving problems regardless of whether they
are doing this for themselves or for their employer.

Some of us can be good at intellectual curiosity but are misers
when it comes to empathic or self-reflective curiosity. There
is no guarantee that if we are good at one, then we are automatically also good at all dimensions of curiosity. We might
be curious at work while the curiosity spark at home with
our significant other has died out.

When James Allan—friend, former colleague, and now head
of part of the shared services organization at Philip Morris
International—received his individual curiosity scale diagnostic report from me, he was surprised. He believed he
would not score very high. His expectation of not scoring

high on intellectual curiosity proved to be correct, yet he aced empathic curiosity. He thrives on being with people and his team appreciates him for the human touch he brings to the table.

While surveying over three thousand professionals globally, I have found senior executives typically score high on cognitive and empathic curiosity, yet their self-reflective curiosity is, on average, lower than their team members. Some people have even coined an uncanny name for this: "CEO disease" (Byrne 1991).

According to this theory, the higher up people are on the organization chart, the more they are separated from reality and only think they are aware of what is going on, while in reality, they don't. Their teams put them on a pedestal of power and might. Employees expect the leader to have answers to difficult questions. Powerful people are thought to be infallible, always right and all-knowing. This aura breeds a feeling of being right, not one of reflection and humility that one can be wrong. The moment leaders conform to this image, they stop being critical about themselves and lose touch with reality.

EMPATHIC CURIOSITY

Human beings are social creatures. The degree to which a person feels a sense of belonging has a big influence on how fulfilled they are at work and more generally in life. As humans, we are intrigued by and gravitate toward others for a host of social benefits: comfort, excitement, emotional support, and so on. Even stronger, interest in how other people behave, think, and feel is a fundamental prerequisite of human relationships. Other people can be defined both as the people we know well—e.g., family, friends, and colleagues—as well as complete strangers.

Social or empathic curiosity is the level of openness we have toward others, their thoughts, and their feelings. It explains how much we are interested in what other people think and feel. It is an indication about how open we are to ideas, emotions, and reactions from others. It investigates our capacity for empathy and how much we can understand the point of view of others.

The better we are at this, the more appreciation we have for others, we feel more related, have more empathy, experience more connectedness, and are generally more engaged in social life.

A powerful case of the power of empathic curiosity can be found in the following story. A modern-day hero of mine is the Vietnamese Buddhist monk Thich Nhat Hanh. In his book *The Art of Living*, he describes how he used his compassionate curiosity with a girl who was raped by a fisherman. He explains he thinks about the girl in his meditation, tries to put himself in the mind of the girl, and sends her compassion. What he does next might seem strange at first. After meditating compassionately with the girl in mind, he then focuses on the fisherman and performs the same compassionate routine. He explains the fisherman also needs to be supported, saved, and sent love (Nhat Hanh 2017).

I sometimes think of this case when thinking of George Floyd, the African American who was killed by a policeman in Minneapolis. On May 25, 2021, Mr. Floyd died after being handcuffed and pinned to the ground under the knee of the policeman for more than nine minutes. Many of us sent love in one form or other to George Floyd. Many were sending hate to the policeman. Thich Nhat Hanh would have also sent him love.

That empathic curiosity requires authentic effort and is highlighted by the following rule of thumb:

I don't like this person; I must get to know him better.

It was a rule the American president Abraham Lincoln tried to live by. When he found himself not liking a particular individual, he didn't firm up on his position of dislike or judgment. Rather, he sought to get to know the person better (Rodenhizer 2019).

It takes guts to walk up to someone different from us and start a conversation. How often do we arrange a lunch with a colleague who holds different views from ours? When we expose ourselves to someone (or something) new, the upside to our own growth is so much higher compared to constantly keeping the company of only like-minded people.

I mentioned it is possible to excel at one application of curiosity and not at another. The founder of Eastman Kodak, George Eastman, is a prime example of how multifaceted curiosity can be, and how excelling at one does not automatically equate to excelling at all. George Eastman is reported not to have been particularly good at interpersonal curiosity. Though his intellectual curiosity was running on overdrive, his empathic curiosity was low. He was not well-liked among employees. It is reported his office was near the women's bathroom. If they made too many trips, they would feel his disapproving gaze. He expected the office boy to sharpen pencils in a particular way and instructed janitors on the right way to use a broom. He rarely gave praise and was quick to criticize people around him (Eastman 2015).

When people are good at empathic curiosity, they are genuinely interested in what people think and in their ideas. They are equally good at putting themselves in other people's shoes and try to understand people's emotions and reactions. People who score high are more likely to be intrinsically motivated to engage with people and to learn new things through social interaction. They have a strong willingness to listen to what other people have to say and are willing to share information they possess.

INTRAPERSONAL CURIOSITY

The object of our interest in intrapersonal curiosity is not the external environment but our inner selves. The more we know ourselves, the better we can face the world, the better we can change ourselves, and the more at ease we are in being with others. Through various acts of conscious and purposeful self-reflection, we inspect and evaluate our thoughts, feelings, behaviors, and insights. When we are good at this, we become a better version of ourselves. Laozi described in the *Tao Te Ching* twenty-six hundred years ago:

> "He who knows others is wise. He who knows himself
> is enlightened."
>
> —*Tao Te Ching*, ch. 33

Think you know yourself well?

The truth is only 10 to 15 percent of adults are able to dig through layers and filters of self-talk, opinions, and assumptions to get to who they really are at the core. In the words of Tasha Eurich, self-awareness researcher, "There are two kinds of people, those people who think they are self-aware and those who are" (Eurich 2017).

The German writer Hermann Hesse goes further in his 1919 masterpiece *Demian* when he writes, "Alas, I know this now: man hates nothing in the world more than to walk the road that leads him to himself." It is not only hard for people to become self-aware, but also, we intentionally avoid digging in our souls, fearing we might find something we don't like.

However, the better we are at analyzing our deeper drivers, the better we can identify and express our feelings as well as observe and change our behaviors. Methods to hone this dimension are intensive self-reflection, mindfulness, meditation, and coaching conversations.

Curiosity about ourselves refers to the desire to understand our deeper drivers, purpose, values, and beliefs, to be in tune with our inner self. It is recognized as the degree of self-consciousness we possess. It also relates to our ability to be self-aware of strengths, uplifting and limiting beliefs and blind spots. The better we are at this, the more we are calm, self-aware, resilient, grounded, content, and authentic. Once we are good at it, the easier it is to self-regulate, set proactive goals for ourselves, act on them, monitor progress, and deliver success for ourselves.

Further, people who score high on self-reflective curiosity tend to possess a stable and grounded frame of mind. They are not easily swayed off their feet. They recognize the importance of self-reflection of looking under the personal hood and exploring conscious and unconscious trends. Simultaneously, they have a regular habit of reflection, and given that is important for them, they find time to engage with it.

Reflection can take different forms. It can be a short mental break at work. It can be a stroll away from your desk, a walk in the park, a refreshing bath, or a meditation. In an organizational and team setting, this can mean exploring the team values or reflecting on the team culture, deep listening of customer trends and acting on them. The result of this self-reflection is a higher sense of self-awareness and an understanding of which triggers produce which results. The more self-reflective we are, the easier it is for us to change our behavior in areas we want to improve.

These three distinct applications of curiosity are not only relevant for individuals. Larger systems like teams, organizations, and even societies can be analyzed through the lens of these applications.

As we will see in the next part, we will go deeper yet and start specifically to explore the world of work. The role of curiosity is being recognized, and its impact is starting to be felt. I will share examples, cases, and comparative frameworks to understand and reflect on curiosity as it pertains to professionals, leaders, teams, and organizations.

The Big Ideas

Curiosity is not unidimensional; rather, it hides a comprehensive nature behind a single word, a word we use loosely without much thought. It is indeed more complex than we think. That's probably why there is no unified definition among scholars and there are so many shades of meaning in society surrounding curiosity.

Only by better appreciating this comprehensive nature can we do justice in cultivating curiosity in ourselves, our teams, and the organizations we work in. The clearer the concept we have of the scope of curiosity and the better our language in describing this reality with words, the more we can reflect, analyze, celebrate, and change our concept of curiosity.

Curiosity is heavily influenced by stress as well as our tolerance for stress. To explore the world, one must be able to withstand the anxiety of confronting the new, the mysterious, the awkward, and the ambiguous. The better individuals and organizations are at this, the more they will be able to maximize the benefit of curiosity.

A little bit of stress is good and helps curiosity. Too much anxiety, however, leads to paralysis and our curiosity will be stifled at that moment.

There are three important distinctions when approaching curiosity. We can be intellectually curious and be inquisitive about the world, empathically curious and show authentic interest in others, and interpersonally curious and engage in self-reflection about our values, purpose, and beliefs, even our limiting beliefs and biases.

Questions for Reflection

- Which of the three applications of curiosity (intellectual, empathic, intrapersonal) is best/ least developed for you?

- What can you do to strengthen the dimensions you are already good at?

- How resilient are you to stress? How does it impact your showing up curiously?

- Reflect on your earlier definition of curiosity. Has it shifted? How so?

- If you look at your team, how would you rate its intellectual, empathic, and self-reflective capacity for curiosity? Are there areas you can improve upon?

PART TWO

FINDING CURIOUS AGENTS

5

WHAT CURIOUS PROFESSIONALS CAN TEACH US

———

"Curiosity is not only about finding new ideas. It is about being able to deal with the new, the complex. It is about being able and willing to continue even if the new brings unpleasant feelings with it."

—DR. CARL NAUGHTON, BUSINESS PSYCHOLOGIST

AND CURIOSITY RESEARCHER

How is it possible to translate the soul of a country into a restaurant menu? This was the task Virgilio Martínez Véliz set for himself to solve.

Virgilio was born in Lima, Peru, in 1977. When he was young, Virgilio was hyperactive and had difficulty following rules and structure. Peru at that time was dangerous and unstable, and its society was fractured: every region was closed off from each other, and economically, the country was barely surviving. While his friends decided to go to college in Peru, Virgilio felt Peru had nothing to offer. His goal was to travel the world while earning his way through working in kitchens.

In the beginning, cooking was an excuse to travel, then it turned into a passion. In Virgilio's own words, "The first time I stepped in a kitchen, it was an amazing experience. I saw the kitchen and saw this huge energy, the noises, the people, working with my hands, my mind. It was something new. I knew this was my habitat, the place I wanted to be. "

In those days, if you wanted to be a chef, you had to be schooled in the traditional cuisines, from French to Italian to Japanese, and for six years, that's what he did. When he joined the team of Gastón Acurio, Peru's most famous chef, he started to explore Peruvian cuisine. After four years, he started his own restaurant and named it Central. He dreamt about creating a radically new Peruvian cuisine in his own way.

Though initial customer feedback of his own new restaurant was good, Virgilio felt confused. His customers did not think his restaurant was special. Influenced by his international experience, Virgilio realized that just adding a Peruvian touch was not going to help him achieve his goal. His menu lacked identity; he needed to make changes. He traveled for a full year in his own Peru, searching for his country's soul. He found many souls: the soul of the Andes, the Pacific, the coastal desert, and the Amazon. He learned about different people, their beliefs and customs, their landscapes, food, and ingredients, and he always asked himself the question: "How can I replicate this in my restaurant?"

He had an epiphany when he learned the people high up in the Andes believe the world is vertical and not horizontal. He decided to recreate his menu according to the different levels of altitudes and different landscapes, making sure every dish became a painting of that altitude and landscape. He wanted people to feel these different parts of Peru. He set out to explore the unique ingredients from each distinct ecosystem and then found a way to combine them on a plate together.

His first dish was called "spiders on a rock." The inspiration came from a low altitude trip to the seaside.

In Virgilio's own words: "It was a beautiful scene. All these little crabs walking on the rock. I saw the whole ecosystem of this rock. These ingredients are sharing the same soil, the same environment, the same ecosystem. I thought if we put them together back in our kitchen, it could work."

In this dish, he recreated the rock scene and combined the different ingredients like the crab, the limpet, and the algae onto a single plate.

He realized by reinventing his approach to food that he might actually lose his customer base at that time. Losing customers, however, did not deter him: "I was so obsessed about achieving this idea of showing Peru in a vertical way that I knew I had to follow my heart." In 2012, he launched his menu uniquely based on altitude with twenty distinct dishes. Nobody had done this before. Suddenly, everybody started to pay attention.

Within one year, in 2012, his restaurant entered The World's 50 Best Restaurants List. One year later, he became number four. He has remained in this competitive top ten list ever since.

Virgilio is still pursuing his dream and exploring new and previously unknown ingredients, yet within the same paradigm: "At Central, we want to show you Peru in a vertical way. You can experience dishes where you first experience the Andes, and then you go to the sea for a second course, then going up the valleys, then you are crossing over to the Amazonia, you can go to as many as seventeen ecosystems in one single dining experience."

From the above story, we can distill that curious people tend to be:

- Open to novelty

- Interested in a challenge

- Willing to take risks in pursuit of a goal

- Hungry for knowledge

- Natural explorers and less afraid of change and new frontiers

- Better at forming deep relationships.

We commonly assign curiosity to children because they are good at joyous exploration and risk taking. They are constantly exploring the world with joyful wonder, driving their parents mad with incessant questions, and willing to take risks (e.g., to get burned by the light of a candle) in their relentless pursuit of new knowledge.

Adults, on the other hand, are better at prolonged and more disciplined intellectual focus; sometimes the object of curiosity is spanning a longer time horizon or even an entire lifetime, as is the case with Virgilio or the artist Pablo Picasso. Adults also are better at empathic curiosity and can develop self-reflective curiosity better than kids, even though not all adults explore this aspect of curiosity.

In the workplace, curious professionals differ from their incurious counterparts in terms of: job satisfaction, engagement at work, commitment, learning agility, idea generation, and innovation.

Indeed, the relevance to organizations of curious employees is apparent: curious employees are responding better to fast-changing environments in the modern workplace by learning faster and by being more intrigued than frustrated when trying to proactively understand the changes affecting them.

They are keen to extract the unique value of new situations, colleagues, and technologies and are more flexible in dealing with unfamiliar cultures in global settings and dealing more easily with uncertainty. As for improving work performance, curious employees are more apt to proactively seek feedback, ask open-ended questions during the acquisition of feedback, and effectively cope with ambivalent feedback from coworkers and supervisors.

I was introduced to Virgilio via two ways. My son dropped out of school and became passionate about cooking. He first learned French cuisine and then worked under the mentorship of a once Michelin-two-star chef in Antwerp, Belgium. Hungry to explore more, he enrolled in a six-month course in Tokyo to learn Japanese cuisine, and then did a couple of short traineeships with renowned fine dining restaurants like Azurmendi in Spain. He told me Peru was one of the key upcoming countries to watch in the world of fine dining. He did not go there in the end, yet an indirect result was I got primed in making a positive connection between Peru and good food.

A second and more detailed introduction happened by Anai "Ani" von Merck, change and transformation expert for PepsiCo based out of Lima. I had done some curiosity work for PepsiCo University and was invited to mentor Ani on a project to create a curiosity curriculum for PepsiCo globally. It was Ani who introduced me to Virgilio and the documentary in the *Chef's Table* series on Netflix about him.

THE RISE OF THE CURIOUS PROFESSIONAL

Some people are naturally more curious than others. Nowadays, being curious is more and more socially accepted for professionals. Times have been different. Until the 1950s, curiosity was seen as a characteristic of nosy and pushy people (Berlyne 1978).

Not anymore. Now more and more employers are valuing and searching for curious professionals. Not only start-ups— Merck KGaA, Darmstadt, Germany uses curiosity proactively in their recruiting campaigns and advises candidates in their recruitment value proposition that they can "bring curiosity to life" once they join the company. Pratt & Whitney also center their recruitment approach around curiosity for instance when they expanded operations in India.

Most employers might not be intentional about curiosity in their job postings or interview strategies, yet it is fair to say curious professionals are increasingly in demand. Employers are looking for people who can do more than follow procedures blindly or who only get going when triggered by a manager. Employers have come to appreciate individuals with a strong intrinsic desire to learn, solve complex problems, challenge the status quo, and ask pertinent questions internally and of customers.

In the workplace, curious professionals differ from their incurious counterparts in terms of job satisfaction, work engagement, commitment, change readiness, learning agility, healthy work relationships, idea generation, and innovation. Indeed, the relevance to organizations of curious employees is apparent. In times of crisis, curious employees are responding better to fast-changing environments in the modern workplace.

Curious individuals at work are more intrigued than frustrated when trying to understand, appreciate, and extract the unique value of new situations, colleagues, and technologies and are more flexible in dealing with unfamiliar cultures in global settings and uncertainty. Curious professionals ask how change can work for them. Less curious people are more prone to being anxious in the face of change, feel paralyzed, try to block out the change, stop exploring, and defend the status quo.

Curious employees are reported as having a better tolerance for stress, which correlates directly with higher job satisfaction and lower employee turnover. Such employees tend to be more willing to seek feedback, ask open-ended questions while receiving feedback, and effectively embrace both critical and constructive feedback from coworkers and supervisors. They are fearless when it comes to embarking upon an extended investigation to find answers to deeply rooted questions.

In sales, research has found it is the "challenger" salesperson who gets more respect from customers versus the incurious salesperson who goes with the flow and as a result sells more. Being curious, proactively probing, and co-creating meaning by asking difficult questions in complex projects gets more business (Dixon 2011).

Such curious professionals might be difficult to manage at times, for they don't respond well to quiet conformity and still compliance being told what to do. They might have different points of view than their superiors. If managed well, however, they will be worth the difficulty.

Curious professionals go deep, and they go wide. They are the people best equipped for the kind of knowledge-rich, mentally challenging work required in complex environments like… pretty much every single industry. They are the ones who can go both deep into their specialization, and also make creative connections between disparate fields. The kind of connections that lead to new solutions and innovation. At a basic level, curious people are aware of what they need to progress; they know they don't have the info, and they are willing to find the missing information.

Curious professionals are the ones whose jobs are least likely to be taken by intelligent machines. In the present time and place, it is no longer sufficient to have a degree and be smart. Computers are smart. Computers are, however, not curious.

A CURIOUS PROFESSIONAL IS MORE LIKELY TO...

As long as I can remember, I have been a curious person. As a young boy, I devoured books so much, my sister made fun of me. I was drawn to reading because I loved new knowledge; I was also looking for a safe place to hide as my social skills needed more development. When I turned fifteen, I started taking evening classes in modern Greek. For those who think of me as a nerd, you are probably right, albeit that same year I also joined the boy scouts, which helped me develop some much-needed social skills. These social skills helped when I embarked on a two-and-a-half-month solo hitch-hiking trip through Europe when I was seventeen. This was just before I entered university.

Since then, I have lived and worked in nine countries (France, Hong Kong, China, Finland, Belgium, the Netherlands, India, Saudi Arabia, and the United Kingdom). I started in investment consulting on the back of a master's thesis on pre-contractual problems of sino-foreign joint ventures in China. From there I set up the executive education arm of a business school in Shanghai. Post this, I moved fulltime in learning and development and drove employee education, customer education, learning innovation, strategy, and implementation for companies such as Nokia, Philips, Agfa, Flipkart, and Cognizant. Prior to founding the Global Curiosity Institute, I oversaw global talent development of the three hundred thousand employees at the IT services company Cognizant as their chief learning officer.

I say I am curious with some hesitation. Self-professing a positive mindset is hardly a good strategy. The real curious individuals don't boast that they are curious. The Chinese Philosopher Laozi once said, "Those who know do not speak; those who speak do not know."

Humility is one of the traits of curious individuals. Sri Sri Ravi Shankar, an Indian modern-day mystic, spoke once about discipline. He warns against labelling oneself as "disciplined," or in our case "curious," indicating the moment we label ourselves, we indicate we achieved mastery and stop trying (Shankar 2021).

I will, therefore, leave it up to you to decide whether I am a curious individual. To give you some extra information, I am someone who does not settle for the status quo, someone who has kept some of his youthful playfulness in exploring different countries, companies, and challenges. I speak six languages. Unlike my antisocial start early on, I now thrive when I am around people. My first impulse is to ask questions. Not so much the type of incurious closed questions only asking for a yes or a no. I prefer open questions where the answer is not binary but can go in any direction. I also like to ideate and turn ideas into reality; I know I don't have all the answers and neither do I have all the questions.

When asking over five hundred professionals in sixteen companies how a curious person is more likely to behave at work, I discerned the following results:

A curious professional is more likely to...

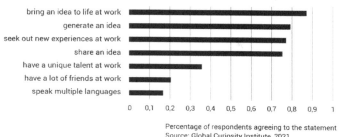

Percentage of respondents agreeing to the statement
Source: Global Curiosity Institute, 2021

The data in this graph makes sense: Curiosity is linked to generating ideas, sharing them, and bringing them to life at work. Curious professionals also want to seek out new experiences at work. It is less linked to having talent, having friends, or speaking multiple languages.

Interestingly, when digging a bit deeper, this graph hides some extra wisdom: men assign a higher value to curiosity and "having a talent" than women. People under the age of thirty link curiosity more to having friends than their older colleagues do. In countries where more than one official language is spoken, such as Belgium or Canada, speaking multiple languages suddenly becomes more important as a dimension of curiosity.

Virgilio fits this profile of the curious professional well. He excelled in bringing his dream to life and created a menu based on altitudes. He traveled the world and then his own country in search of its different characteristics. In other words, he was trying to make meaning out of the various experiences he had and kept asking how he could transform these experiences in his restaurant.

Though clearly very talented in his craft of cooking, he has a certain humility about him. He continues to be curious, exploring the culinary world to keep digging into cooking and searching for the undiscovered ingredients in every part of Peru.

"I realized we know nothing, Yeah, we know a little, that's it. And I am still learning a lot. This is a work in progress. This is just the beginning."
—VIRGILIO MARTÍNEZ VÉLIZ

CURIOUS PROFESSIONALS LEARN BETTER, FASTER, AND DEEPER

For individuals, curiosity is a fundamental human motivation that influences learning, the acquisition of knowledge, and life fulfillment. Being a state of active interest, curiosity creates an openness to unfamiliar experiences, laying the groundwork for greater opportunities to emerge and experience. My own research has indicated curious individuals tend to advance more quickly in their careers and earn more money faster than others.

A growing body of research shows us curiosity makes us better professionals. We know intuitively, for instance, curiosity correlates positively with learning. The more curious you are about something, the more motivated you will be to find out more about it.

Researchers have found an interesting additional feature of curiosity. When our curiosity piques, our brain is automatically primed to retain new information better—any information, even information that has no relevance to what sparked our curiosity in the first place (Gruber 2019).

When we are in a curious frame of mind, we learn faster and better any piece of information that comes our way. In such cases, it is as if our entire brain primes itself positively to receive new information. In such a state, both our short-term and long-term memory work better. Who does not remember the teacher whose passion was so addictive; the entire class also became interested? As it happens, in this state, we were also more open to the next class as we were primed to welcome any new information.

This underscores why it is so important for organizations to give people freedom to set and pursue their own learning goals. Once employees decide on a learning goal themselves (instead of being told what and when to learn), they will take learning more seriously, learn faster and remember what they learn better.

In practice, companies who are good at empowering employees in pursuing their own learning goals often find the right balance between what learning is required for the role and allowing employees to explore learning on their own. Having employees pull the knowledge and training they feel they need is more effective than ordering them to take a class they do not see the value in taking.

THE DIFFERENCE BETWEEN CURIOUS
AND INCURIOUS PROFESSIONALS

Ulrik Juul Christensen, founder and chief executive officer at Area9, a successful next-generation learning technology company, explored with me the traits of curious people. We used his own experience as a lens to come up with some of the dimensions which define curious professionals.

- **They are interested in getting good at things**. According to Mr. Christensen, a lot of people could get good at a lot more things if only they would have a different mindset. Wanting to get good (or better) at things can be explained as the difference between a fixed mindset and a growth mindset. Do you think you can improve, or do you think you have to deal with some pre-dealt cards given at the beginning of your life?

- **They are not afraid to make mistakes**. Curious professionals are often top performers, as they will not subscribe to the common phrase: "curiosity killed the cat." Mr. Christensen affirms, "It is the other way around: it is the lack of curiosity that kills the cat."

- **They are playful**: He uses the analogy of one of his mentees: Viktor Axelsen, the Danish Olympic champion and world number-one in badminton. Viktor would often intentionally try to do silly things during his long training sessions. Most of the time, these silly moves don't work, yet sometimes they do. He then matures these moves and uses them to his advantage in competition. His willingness to not settle for the status quo but try new things out and be a constant novice, be humble to know that there is more to learn and explore even for an Olympic champion. Experimentation is at the heart of his success. An important caveat Mr. Christensen shares is the following: it is not just playfulness; it is disciplined and deliberate playfulness driven by natural curiosity. Most professionals in sports and at work share this trait. As a side remark, we discussed jokingly there would be probably one exception to this in the world of sports. John McEnroe thought he was so talented, everything that did not go his way was somebody else's fault.

- **They are more interested in the process than the result**. He articulated something I observed with many other successful professionals: "I have never been interested in accomplishments; I have always been interested in understanding the deeper why and solving problems."

- **They have a sense of urgency**. For curious professionals, curiosity is a pressure release valve, a necessity which, if not satisfied, leads to boredom. Curious professionals see curiosity as something that requires being treated as importance and urgency.

I have come to know Mr. Christensen over several years or so and have found more elements which accentuate his curious nature. Being at the forefront of technology, he offers summer jobs to fifteen- to seventeen-year-olds every year to reverse mentor him on how he could improve his adaptive learning platform. I can attest to this as he invited my sixteen-year-old son to review some of his online adaptive courses and critique them.

He is also a scuba diving fanatic. Not just an amateur, he has achieved mastery and holds the rank of scuba diving instructor. He is also generous with his time in mentoring and coaching people. He also was the first one to open his company to do a company-wide scan exploring both the individual curiosity levels of his entire team and measuring how well his company's culture, processes, and practices were enabling curiosity. Many executives prefer not to know as they might hear things they don't want to hear. Mr. Christensen welcomed my organizational curiosity assessment with open arms.

When coming up with a structured difference between curious professionals and their incurious peers, the following differences can be distilled.

Curious versus incurious professionals

INCURIOUS PROFESSIONALS	CURIOUS PROFESSIONALS
Rely on being perceived as expert	Are comfortable to be a constant novice
Skim the surface	Go deep and broad
Are incidental learners	Are constant learners
Adopt a fixed mindset	Embrace a growth mindset
Are reactive and closed	Are proactive and open
Rely on past knowledge	Takes time and responsibility to keep up with business and colleagues
Are dependent on environment	Create the environment

As do many others, Ulrik Juul Christensen and Virgilio Martínez Véliz exemplify the curious professional.

Dr. Yury Boshyk, founder and CEO of Global Executive Learning and Business Driven Action Learning (BDAL), added to this list of traits of curious professionals when I spoke to him. According to him, curious professionals:

- Excel in asking lots of open-ended questions.

- Are learning faster and greater than the rate of change around them.

- Are willing to get outside of their comfort zone and are fine with dealing with unfamiliar settings, novel problems, and new colleagues.

We agreed, asking questions is one of the most difficult things for executives to do. Leaders are paid to solve things, to have an opinion, to share their knowledge. In many organizations, most executives will ask closed questions that most often elicit "yes" or "no" responses. Leaders and professionals can, however, be taught to be more curious and learn to ask better open-ended questions.

To conclude with Virgilio's story, at no time is he afraid to embark on a new journey: leave Peru, set up his restaurant business, or change its course. He is open to learning new things and deepening the paths he has laid out in the past. Yet he is not afraid to try new approaches. He is aware of the limitations of his own capabilities. For him to be able to focus on exploration, he relies on his sister, Malena, to run the structured research arm of his restaurant and his wife oversees the kitchen and turning his innovation ideas into action.

A PROFESSIONAL'S GUIDE TO DEVELOPING CURIOSITY

The strategies I suggest here are meant as a reflection moment. If you want to explore improvement strategies more, I suggest you visit the chapter on architecting curiosity at the end of this book.

- Plan for curiosity.

- Engage in effortful and intentional curiosity.

- Build knowledge.

- Surround yourself with curious people.

- Surprise yourself: have lunch (or have an online meeting) with that new colleague or buy the book next to the one you wanted to buy.

- Make a habit of exploring something new (or learn something new).

- Explore your deeper self and values.

In the next chapter, we will look at the enormous influence leaders have in either uplifting or stifling the team. It is time for the curious leaders to be celebrated and recognized. The best leaders are those who create the conditions in which curious professionals can thrive.

The Big Ideas

Curious professionals differ from their more incurious peers and display a set of behaviors. In the workplace, curious professionals display positive attitudes toward work in terms of job satisfaction, engagement at work, commitment, learning agility, idea generation, and innovation.

Professionals who are high on curiosity are more likely to generate and share ideas, yet they don't stop there. They are also good at implementing ideas and are always looking for new experiences. They learn better, faster, and deeper.

Curiosity can be taught; with the right effortful activity, companies can influence the curiosity levels of their employees. Depending on the right focus and the right environment, curiosity is like a muscle that can be trained and made stronger. It all depends on intentional activity.

Questions for Reflection

- How intentional and consistent are you with regard to your curiosity?

- When looking at the list of curious versus incurious professionals, where you are on each dimension?

- When was the last time you got good at something new?

- How much do you focus on rejuvenating yourself: intellectually, physically, and spiritually?

- How much are you uplifting others with your curiosity?

6

WHAT CURIOUS
LEADERS ACTUALLY DO

———

"Before you are a leader, success is all about growing yourself. When you become a leader, success is all about growing others."

—JACK WELCH

Is it true, leadership is hard and curious leaders are hard to come by? Is it possible we are pursuing an outdated leadership style?

THE SPRINGBOKS

On June 24, 1995, the Springboks won the Rugby World Cup. Tension was high in Johannesburg; the new democratic South African nation had just been formed under the charismatic leadership of Nelson Mandela. It had been barely one year since Mandela was in office. All South Africans were only gradually getting used to the new order in the country as

Apartheid had been dismantled. A new wind was blowing in the country affecting all layers of society. Mandela was looking for symbols to heal his country. One of these symbols was rugby. Mandela's inspiring leadership helped inspire South Africa's national rugby team to win the 1995 Rugby World Cup and brought many South Africans, Black and White, together in the process.

It was not easy. The newly elected president had to overcome two challenges. First, he needed to ensure the team itself regained a positive belief in their capacity to be convinced they could do better. Indeed, prior to the World Cup in 1995, the Springboks were only in ninth place on the global ranking and were not expected to dethrone the incumbent champions of Australia, who had not lost a game in the preceding twelve months (Evans 2021).

Second, he had to convince his Black constituency not to dismantle the Springbok team, which was composed primarily of white players, but let them compete. This was a controversial decision as the team had been a symbol of Apartheid. Even its name "Springbok," meaning gazelle in English, was a word from Afrikaans, the language of the South African White minority.

Faced with these challenges, Nelson Mandela set and clarified a compelling vision and strategy, stretched the team to achieve a goal they did not think possible, and above all created psychological safety for the team. He also led the team with a remarkable curiosity, grounded in deep self-awareness. He displayed a deep empathic curiosity to the players and visited them at training. Particularly, he mentored the team's captain: François Pienaar to believe in himself and uplift the team. He also displayed a more than average cognitive curiosity to raise the ante for his country (Evans 2021).

AMBIDEXTERITY

It is hard to be an exceptional leader, regardless of whether you are high up in the executive arena, running a fragile country like Mandela, or whether you are a frontline manager. Forget "exceptional"—it is hard to be a good leader.

It is also hard to find good leaders. Wout Van Impe and Nicolas Alaerts from leadership and executive recruitment company Mercuri Urval shared with me an interesting fact when interviewing them: a large percentage of executive placements seem to fail.

An extensive 2015 internal study of twenty thousand executive placements was conducted by the executive search firm Heidrich and Struggles. The study revealed 40 percent of the executives fail within eighteen months. A failure means the executive left, was asked to leave, or was performing significantly below expectations (Moss 2017). Consistent with data from other research in subsequent years, the success of executive appointments was no better than 50 percent. Executive recruitment seems to be a hit-or-miss activity. Candidates have an equal chance to succeed or fail. (Moore 2021). This is one of the reasons why specialists like Wout Van Impe and Nicolas Alaerts are rethinking executive recruitment strategies with their clients.

What is then a curious leader?

Curious leaders invite ideas from their teams and create the right trusting environment where asking questions, even dissenting ones, is encouraged and celebrated. They are role models and are successful at driving changes given that they are curious individuals themselves. Curious leaders don't behave as if they know everything and as if they are the locus of knowledge. Instead, they have and promote a disposition toward acknowledging they don't have all the answers yet are curious to find them together with the team.

The challenges managers face today are less predictable than they were in the last century. Solutions to problems are less driven by the past and the power to effect change requires more gentle influence than formal top-down authority. A great deal of leadership energy goes into predicting the future and trying to create stability.

Leadership is ambidextrous. Leaders need to be good at keeping their ship afloat while, at the same time, reinventing the future. In the strategic literature, this is referred to as exploitation and exploration. Curiosity in its various dimensions is well suited to assist leaders to widen their perspectives, listen intently, engage new challenges, experiment, and learn faster, and build organizations that create results in times of crisis. Managers can create the right circumstances for the employee, make sure the employee has the right knowledge and tools, and the right psychological safety to perform well on the job, and explore how they themselves can improve as well as come up with ideas of how the team can get better.

Like Mandela, leaders find themselves in turbulent situations. The better leaders are confident to try out a few things and to be brave. Embedded in the core of leadership behavior is the need for leaders to engage in trial and error and experimentation. Engagement, not simply trying to analytically study the problem from a distance, leads to fostering success and killing failures when they arise. Curiosity is an attribute for leaders to adapt and succeed.

WHAT MAKES A CURIOUS LEADER?

A useful way to describe a curious leader is to explore its opposite. In workshops with leaders, I often begin by asking the group what they consider a curious leader is not. Invariably: people throw up concepts like rigid, closed-minded, autocratic, selfish, old-fashioned, top-down, conformist, goes with the flow....

These intuitive replies are coming back in research. In a cross-industry curiosity study led by curiosity researcher Todd Kashdan, the report posits several curiosity barriers associated with leaders (Merck 2016).

1. Autocratic, top-down leadership behavior stifles curiosity as curious subordinates are not provided with the opportunity to question or challenge decisions, nor are they invited to explore and share novel options.

2. The prevalence of risk-averse behavior makes leaders opt for proven and safe ideas, thus restricting creative thinking time.

3. A preference for conformity and fear of standing out from others among managerial peers.

The above points already highlight several dimensions explaining incurious leadership behavior. What also becomes clear is leadership positions are sensitive to the nature/nurture divide. Leaders show up with their own level of curiosity, yet simultaneously are also adapting their individual inclination for curiosity to the context they are in.

To prove the latter point: my research has revealed, when looking at frontline, mid-level, and senior leaders, there is a different appreciation of workplace curiosity among these leader groups. I found mid-level managers are four times less excited about curiosity when compared to their junior or senior peers. This is not entirely surprising. In most organizations, mid-level managers are tasked with implementing the strategic goals as set by senior management in the most efficient manner. Experimentation with novel—yet unproven—ways of reaching their targets is often the last thing on their mind.

For mid-level managers, the downside of taking risks is greater than the upside. When things go south and the risks are prone to become failures, the direct results are limiting career mobility and lower financial gain. First line managers, on the other hand, enjoy relatively more freedom in operational matters.

Comparison of curious versus incurious leaders

INCURIOUS LEADERS	CURIOUS LEADERS
Stifle curiosity	Authorize curiosity
Have know-it-all mentality	Have a learn-it-all mentality
Give feedback	Give and ask for feedback
Are only focused on their functional specialty	Focus on both functional specialty as well as broader topics
Position themselves above the team	Are in the team: physically, mentally, emotionally and spiritually
Go with the flow	See and clarify a compelling vision and challenge
Avoid failure at all costs	Celebrate first-time failures as a source of learning
Display a fixed mindset	Have situational fluency: can read and influence the context
Have difficulty describing personal values	Live by clear values
Focus on efficiency	Balance efficiency and curiosity
Listen with an intention to fix	Listen with an intention to learn

When we zoom in to the last point in the table, we observe the power of listening for leaders. You might argue that is common sense, yet as we can see, it is not always common practice. Listening has many shades. The least useful shade is listening with the intention to fix. This is a selfish type of listening as the focus is on closed questions and confirmation of the beliefs of the listener and not the speaker.

A better listening strategy is one where the listener focuses on the speaker, asks open questions with the intention of learning. The best strategy is the one where maximum awareness and intuition come into play, and where there is also a focus on what is not said.

When teaching leadership earlier in my career, I often used the Chinese word for listening, "ting," as a metaphor. There are two ways to write this character, either in the simplified or the classical version. The modern simplified version stresses the way the character is built "listening in order to speak." The classical version on the other hand describes the holistic nature of listening: it represents the act of listening being executed with both the heart and the ears, giving undivided focus in the process, and treating the other person as a king.

Curious leaders give undivided attention and are mindful in the moment when communicating with others. How good is your listening?

THE POSITIVE SHADOW OF A LEADER

We established earlier, the productive curiosity of the CEO leads to both an increase in the operational efficiency of the company and greater openness to exploring new things. When the CEO, or the team leader for that matter, is high on curiosity, the members of the organization are more likely to agree with the statement that the organization encourages curiosity. This does not mean employees at all levels of the organization automatically feel encouraged and enabled to show up curiously at work. Next to being role models, leaders also need to establish habits and interactions, so employees are reassured curiosity is not reserved for people at the top.

Curiosity needs champions. The shadow the manager casts is an important driver for team curiosity. In my own research, I have established a linear correlation between the numbers of hours a manager spends on the acquisition of new information and knowledge through reading books or articles, viewing educational videos and taking (e-) classes, listening to podcasts or e-books, and so on. The more the manager consumes new knowledge, the more the team also follows in the curious behavioral footsteps of the leader. As a result, there is an increase in the hours the team spends on learning to mimic those of the leader. Intuitively this makes sense. When the manager is curious herself, she will—openly or not—make it clear she values new knowledge in the team. The team will recognize that learning and intellectual exploration is important and will follow her example.

The inverse is sadly also true. If a manager does not communicate in words or—more importantly in actions—that learning is important, the team refrains from consuming learning. Luckily, not all team members mimic the manager's learning habits. Some of them—the A players—are intrinsically so curious, even a non-conducive environment does not stop them from exploring. A-players are not negatively influenced by the behavior of their leader. What is clear is: good managers uplift the team and stretch it beyond what they thought was feasible. Bad managers, on the other hand, stifle the team and hold it back.

Simon Brown, the chief learning officer at Novartis, shared with me a similar telling statistic when I interviewed him. In their internal annual engagement surveys, they found an excellent people manager scores on average three percentage points better than the average manager. Bad managers score a staggering eighteen points lower on overall team engagement and twenty-two points lower on curiosity. For Novartis, a bad manager gets about six times more negative feedback than an excellent one gets good feedback. People penalize their incurious leaders in surveys and give little credit to those who do well.

To my knowledge, few companies are actively measuring the effectiveness of their leaders, even fewer companies are proactively training and coaching all leaders receiving critical scores from their teams.

That the daily actions of leaders affect team members has been researched by Spencer Harrison, associate professor of organizational behavior at INSEAD. Professor Harrison studied the daily logs of teams of scientists working in desert-based Mars simulators. He used linguistic text analysis of team leads and checked how often question marks (an indicator of asking questions) were used, as well as exclamation points (a reflection of surprise).

He then correlated this to the logs of the team members in terms of their use of curious language: simply put whether the team members used words like "invent," "create," "discover," "new," "novel," "different," etc. He found a standard deviation in question marks and/or exclamation points the day before also led to a change in standard deviation of the use of curious words of the team members the day after (Harrison 2021).

A 2018 groundbreaking study of three thousand international employees conducted by the Harvard Business

School professor Francesca Gino disclosed the implications of workplace curiosity and the corresponding leadership support for curiosity. She states curiosity is an important aspect of a company's performance because of the following reasons:

1. When curiosity is triggered, leaders tend to be more intentional and rational about their decision making.

2. Curiosity makes leaders—and their teams—more adaptable to the dynamics of uncertain market environments.

3. Curious leaders command higher levels of respect of their followers than incurious leaders (Gino 2018).

Workplace curiosity works in real time. When leaders are more curious and invite surprise about everyday activities, the more it has a carry-over effect on team members.

CONFLICTING MANAGERIAL BEHAVIOR

That innovation is good for an organization—engaged employees perform better, curious individuals suggest ideas and bring ideas to life, and enabling managers uplift the team are all accepted as truisms. With this belief in the back of their mind, many managers also make the illogical jump in asserting their organization is, therefore, also curious.

Common sense does not automatically equate to common practice. A crucial misconception is that curiosity will naturally occur in any reasonably healthy workplace. In fact, curious work environments are rare. They require deliberate and consistent action.

When studying in the above-mentioned Harvard Business School research how leaders viewed curiosity, Professor Francesca Gino found: "Although leaders might say they treasure inquisitive minds, in fact, most stifle curiosity, fearing it will increase risk and inefficiency" (Gino 2018).

This is an important finding, resonating with my own research. On the one hand, executives realize the underlying importance of curiosity in helping to implement their firm's strategy agenda when it comes to product and services innovation, outwitting competition, winning deals, taking calculated risks in the pursuit of novel and creative outcomes, etc. On the other hand, these same executives are rejecting curiosity as something which goes against the grain of operational efficiency of the organization.

I mentioned data to prove this point earlier that 90 percent of leaders believe investing in curiosity to drive innovation is a worthwhile investment, yet when correlating to another question on whether innovation is welcomed in teams, 50 percent of the same executives are worried that spending time on innovation distracts the team from being efficient.

Balesh Raghurajan, director of the India-based consulting company Effilor, rightly pointed out:

> There is a certain fancy associated with sales and winning deals and as a natural effect, leaders expect "exploration" and "creativity" from their sales teams. But when it comes to execution, they look

for compliance and "efficiency," not for improvement ideas. That's why certain departments like sales, marketing, and strategy seem to invite curiosity from their teams while finance, production, legal, and administration are seen as pure efficiency drivers.

Curiosity researcher and leadership consultant Alison Horstmeyer shared an efficiency myth-buster: "A single efficiency focus leads to error avoidance, which means there is limited to no opportunity for exploration and experimentation because you are squarely focused on leveraging and maximizing only what you know and your current resources available to you. Behaviors linked to curiosity such as exploration, experimentation, and informed risk-taking, on the other hand, lead to error management, providing a potent way to increase individual agility and stress tolerance. It also increases organizational flexibility in the short- and long-run. Error avoidance is typically linked to high conformity environments, which have an inverse relationship to openness to change, and subsequently, little tolerance for curiosity."

In a study, one done in collaboration with SurveyMonkey and INSEAD, a discrepancy was highlighted between how corporate leaders perceive their work environment versus the non-managerial population in their companies. What the researchers found was leaders often have a rosier picture of the environment. Eighty-six percent of executives think of their organization as one that supports curiosity while only 52 percent of their team members thought the same (Harrison 2018).

My own research points in the same direction. Leaders are twice as ready to say their company recognizes curious professionals, and curiosity leads to career progression and financial gains when compared to non-leaders.

OLD MINDSETS

What are the reasons for this gap between theoretically endorsing curiosity, yet practically not fully embracing it? To find an answer to this question, we need to lean against our twentieth century industrial management mindsets and explore its associated beliefs.

1. Belief: **Curiosity slows down operational efficiency and detracts the team from strategic focus.** Leaders believe letting the team focus on curiosity will lead to protracted periods of non-productive brainstorming and ideation. Leaders have grown up with the belief perpetuating the past is better than inviting the future and an action mindset is better than a thinking one. As with everything, balance is key: focusing only on perpetuating the tricks of the past with an exploitation mindset will not bear fruit over a longer time, especially when the environment is dynamic. Only exploring without embedding new ideas into operational rigor also does not work. What I have observed is: good leaders know when to allow curiosity, brainstorming, and ideation and when to focus on implementation. Good leaders know that thinking ahead, considering multiple options, and delaying the natural urge to plunge immediately into action can save costs over time. Good leaders also know the combination of an exploratory mindset with an exploitative one is an excellent combination to stay ahead of present and future competition.

2. Belief: **It is better to centralize decision making to manage risks.** Top-down decision making is perceived to be easier than inviting the entire team to collectively build the future. In non-complex environments such as production facilities or support functions, compliance to pre-established processes and procedures is the norm. When confronting a novel situation not previously been encountered, people in power make the decision. In blue-collar workplaces, the reason for this upward delegation of power is often attributed to the high investment value of machinery on the shop floor. Though this financial consideration is important, a deeper belief is hidden underneath: a parent/child concept. (The parent/child concept states: managers are the impersonation of the parent at work and as such are best placed to make decisions.) In this example, blue-collar workers are stereotyped as children. They are thought to lack the required knowledge to engage in new and difficult decisions. To counter this thinking, companies like Toyota and others have proven employee empowerment, even on the blue-collar shop floor where a worker has the authority to stop the assembly line, leads to better operational efficiency (Davis 2019). Companies like Toyota have been adopting agile work methods such as SCRUM, LEAN, and others to facilitate such decentralized decision making.

3. Belief: **The positional power of the leader comes with the burden of knowledge**. Once in power, the leader is supposed to look strong, articulate all questions before the team does, and at the same time have all the answers. Organizational culture often reinforces this

type of belief: the manager has expert status, has all the answers, and is therefore not appreciative of being challenged. When Satya Nadella became CEO at Microsoft in February 2014, one of the first things he did was to change this ingrained culture of "know-it-all" behavior. He replaced it with a culture where "learn-it-all" was the norm, where leaders could admit they did not have all the answers and as a result, invite the entire team to collectively come up with the solution.

4. Belief: **It is better to have followers than challengers**. It is easier for the leader to make a decision and the team to unanimously run with it rather than have the team challenge the decision and explore why it should not work. Even less desirable would be to invite the team to come up with the decision in the first place. Clearly, this mindset errs on the side of groupthink, a psychological situation in teams where the individual members stop asking intelligent questions or challenge the strongest voice but instead follow the leader's decision, even if this decision is a bad one. Groupthink stops people from speaking up.

5. Belief: **Curious people are unruly and are harder to manage**. In the industrial mindset I described above, curiosity is the opposite of compliance or conformity. As such, the preferred employee is the one who follows the rules, does not challenge the manager, and does not ask difficult questions.

WHAT IS HOLDING MANAGERS BACK?

We don't always find it comfortable to be confronted with our own blind spots. Personally, there are times I feel threatened, yet when I sense this sensation rising within me, I force myself then to listen. I don't see new ideas as a threat, I see them as an enrichment to learn from and grow.

We often are not consciously aware of the positional power we hold, and how a small minority imposes their norms on their community. In some (sub)cultures, this is stronger than others. In the science of cross-cultural management, there is this concept of "power distance." Power distance refers to the acceptance of behavior and practices held by the people in power in the eyes of those who are not in power. The fact a CEO has her own parking spot, big office, and a different (often high) reward package is accepted in high power distance countries like Belgium, France, China, and Malaysia (Hofstede 1983).

In other countries, this is unheard of. When I worked at Nokia's Headquarters in 2001, Jorma Ollila, our CEO at the time, had to queue up for lunch in the cafeteria like all other colleagues. When I moved to Agfa in Belgium, there were two restaurants. One self-service cafeteria on the ground floor for all staff, and one on the top floor for only the execs. Being invited to the executive floor was a much-coveted treat.

In the last forty years or so, our cognitive models of leadership have been challenged quite a few times. Depending on what culture we live in and the industry we are engaged in, we find ourselves in paradigms of two different types of leaders. We distinguish between the type of aggressive white knights who singlehandedly save the day with their superior skills and knowledge and the more servant and authentic leader types. Intellectually, these models make sense, and one is preferred over the other depending on the context, the level of crisis, the prevailing country culture, or mindset of the organization.

On the ground, however, we find many more flavors of leaders. In my career, I have been fortunate to work in multiple industries and multiple countries. In my role of chief learning officer for multiple Fortune 200 companies, I was able to mentor, coach, and observe many managers. What I have distilled is a simple belief: though the management training can help managers improve their people management skills, when things get tough, most of these managers return to an unconscious script of how interpersonal relationships between a senior and a junior are supposed to unfold. Helping managers become aware of this script is much more important than training managers on normative leadership concepts.

This script is created either early in life when we see how our parents treat each other, their kids, people in positions of power, and people lower in the perceived pecking order (e.g. cashiers at the local supermarket), or this script can be generated through experiences with our first managers.

Both examples, parents and the first manager, will create an unconscious script in how power relationships play out. If we were lucky to be influenced by the right role model as examples, we will treat our team with respect, trust, and as equals. If we were less lucky, we would think of the team as a bunch of people who cannot be trusted, need to be treated like kids, and are motivated by instilling fear. Those managers who are self-aware are in a good position to reflect on their own management style and decide changes if they desire so.

Managers might credit parents and earlier managers for inspiration, however, blaming them for managerial incompetence might go too far. The people who came before us nurtured us and left a big mark. Our own nature and the experiences we had in life shape the way we translate these experiences into our relationships with others. Some managers do really well; others don't.

When people are comfortable in their managerial roles, curiosity can thrive; when they are not, curiosity is stifled. For this reason the less fortunate managers might be anxiety driven by fear (imposter syndrome, fear of failure). I have seen in both start-ups as well as traditional established companies the Peter Principle. This principle states that people are promoted often one level higher than their natural capacity. These managers can be too young in their career and given managerial authority because they joined the fast-growing company earlier (the case of start-ups), or in the case of traditional enterprises, excel at a technical role and given a managerial position because the only way "up" is into a management role. I have seen that without proper guidance, coaching, and support, such managers can become insecure, less relaxed with the people in their care, and thus less open to novel triggers around them in the workplace.

One remarkable trait of curious leaders is their ability to ask for feedback. In my research, I have found only 23 percent of the frontline team leads ask for reverse feedback. Assuming 100 percent of all frontline managers engage in some form of performance feedback, this means 77 percent fail to ask their team members how well they are doing themselves.

Why is this?

Insecurity and perceived power distance will likely be the main reasons. When the person in power, the manager, is being vulnerable for a moment and asks two simple questions: "How am I doing?" and "How can I become a better version of myself?" Instead of opening to such a learning opportunity, 77 percent of managers chose not to let their subordinates give needed feedback.

Once managers are among each other, when managers higher up are giving feedback to more junior managers in their care, the number doubles to 46 percent. This is already a better number though still indicates many leaders prefer not to ask the people in their care how well they are performing themselves.

Another reason why most frontline managers are incurious about their own performance from the mouths of their team members could be related to a concept called "social stereotyping." It is well established in psychology that people possess well-articulated and engrained social schemata when dealing with others. In interacting with others, we often automatically assume things about—in this case—our team members. The more we stereotype, the more likely we reduce or negate the amount of curiosity toward the thoughts and ideas of others (Loewenstein 1994).

Both insecurity and unconscious social stereotyping are just two dimensions holding leaders back. Nelson Mandela is a good example of a leader who possesses the right level of what I call confident humility. He displays humility when he does not know all the answers yet is okay sharing with others that he does not know and invites others to help solve the issue.

He also engages with people on his team and with Françios Pienaar with openness and empathy.

WHAT LEADERS CAN DO TO GET BETTER AT CURIOSITY

The strategies I suggest here are meant as a reflection moment. If you want to explore improvement strategies more, I suggest you visit the "Architecting Curiosity" chapter at the end of this book.

- Put curiosity on the team agenda.

- Show up as an all-around curious individual interested in the world, the people around you, and yourself.

- Ask for (reverse) feedback.

- Become aware of your question strategies. Are they open-ended or closed?

- Baseline your own curiosity as well as that of the team.

- Identify barriers to curiosity in the team, create quick wins and build on their success.

- Ask the team how they can help in creating a curious environment.

Let's turn next to focus on the traits of curious teams and explore the link between curiosity and high performance at a team level. The role of the leader will remain crucial in creating the right psychological safety environment for the team to show up curiously.

The Big Ideas

The archetype of a curious leader is someone who models curiosity at all levels (intellectually, empathically, and self-reflectively) and who stimulates idea flows within the team and across teams. Curious leaders are both excellent at exploitation as well as exploration; they know when to allow for curiosity and when to drive for action.

Although managers say they treasure inquisitive minds, most, in fact, stifle it. Action is always more important than words or intentions. The shadow a manager casts on her team is paramount in either uplifting the team toward curious heights or stifling the team with conformist expectations.

A curious leader leads with confident humility; she is humble and has the confidence to say so. What is important is the curious leader takes time and responsibility to keep up with the changing reality of customers, business, and each individual team member. Leaders give permission to the team to be curious. They create psychological safety, allowing team members to engage in creative initiatives without the stress of being punished. This is characterized by providing a balanced amount of time and resources and allowing people to make high-volume, low-impact mistakes, which is the best way to learn.

The curious leader displays a willingness to ask questions and actively listen for answers in meetings. She says, "I don't know, so let's find out," or "That's one right answer. What's another one?" She also invites her team members to provide feedback on her own performance: "How well am I (your leader) doing?" "How can I be a better leader?"

One could say the curious leader is embedded in the team and does not see herself above the team. She is respected for going deep into specialist terrains as well as bringing new perspectives to the conversation because of a broad exploration mindset. She stretches the team to levels the team did not expect themselves to achieve. The curious leader focuses on creating a fertile culture in the team where openness, psychological safety and failure acceptance is encouraged. When failure arises, she explains this as a source of learning, not something to be avoided.

Questions for Reflection

If you are a leader,

- How do you lead yourself and others?

- Are you equally inviting exploration next to experimentation into your team? When do you do so? When not?

- What is your reaction when people challenge you: defensiveness or openness?

- How does the table of curious/incurious leaders resonate with you?

- Do you prefer to work more with thinkers/ explorers or doers/implementers?

If you work for a leader,

- How do you describe the curiosity style of your leader?

- What would you like to start/stop and continue in the team when using the lens of curiosity? Discuss with your leader if you deem so appropriate.

- What would you need to achieve to implement your suggestions? (Tip: It is always best to start from a position of strength and trust.)

- If you want to become a leader yourself, how would you approach balancing between curiosity/agility, thinking/doing, and exploitation/exploration?

7

WHY CURIOUS TEAMS ARE SUCCESSFUL

———

"If you want to go quickly, go alone. If you want to go far, go together."

—AFRICAN PROVERB

What does a curious team look like? When we group together several curious people, do we then create an effective curious team?

These were the questions researchers at Google asked themselves.

THE ARISTOTLE PROJECT

Much of the work done at Google, like most organizations, is done collaboratively by teams. The team is the basic unit where real stuff happens, where innovative ideas are conceived and tested, and where employees experience most of their work. But it's also where interpersonal issues, ill-suited skill sets, and unclear group goals can hinder productivity and cause friction.

In 2015, the research team at Google embarked on a journey to find out what the secret is behind successful teams. The logic behind this study was that once they uncovered this, they had a blueprint for successful teams, driving even more successful growth for Google (Duhigg 2016).

Their hypothesis was simple. They wanted to prove the success of the team is tied first and foremost to the sum of individual members of the group, the sum of their individual curiosity, their drive, intelligence, and focus. If this hypothesis holds true, you simply must focus on hiring the right individuals, group these curious, smart, driven energetic individuals together, and you will have created a successful team.

This is a perfectly plausible hypothesis. The individual in most teams and organizations is key to a team's success. The better the individual, the better the team. The researchers at Google worked with 180 teams to prove this hypothesis and tried to find the ideal individual traits of people to bring together to create magic for Google. What they found was quite startling. It was different from what they thought.

They found the overarching whole is more important for a successful team than the sum of its individuals. To their surprise, they discovered what makes a team successful is the overarching culture, climate, processes, and practices. Unique individuals had much less impact on the success of the team. How the environment created a conducive, nurturing environment suddenly proved to be more important than what the individual brought naturally to the table at work. The sum of successful individuals does not equal the success of the team.

Google ended up calling this research project the "Aristotle Project," in tribute to Aristotle's quote: "The whole is greater than the sum of its parts." If you are a curious reader, I am sure you will ask an immediate question, namely: "How much greater?" I had the same question.

CONDITIONS OF CURIOUS TEAMS

We have long realized the environment is an important part in shaping an individual. We have come to call this "nurture." The opposite is "nature." Nature is the concept we are endowed with certain traits at birth. We all agree you need a combination of both. We also have already established healthy human beings have these two dimensions available with equal strength (Tellegen 1988).

In other words, genetics or nature explains about half of the observed differences in personality traits, whereas the other half depends on the environment and experiences we have after we are born to the present day. It is a good thing that not everything is 100 percent fixed at birth. Fifty percent remains flexible, meaning it is possible for individuals to train their curiosity and get better at it.

Ditto for teams. At work, we need both a conducive environment as well as smart, curious, and focused individuals to make things work. As a team, we can also collectively get better at curiosity, provided we invite small changes to the design of our teams.

Can a team be too curious, or can the curiosity become destructive? It can. In psychology, the under-expression of curiosity is depression, and the overexpression is distractibility. When curiosity is not allowed in a team, it leads to a negative state. At that moment, people stop showing interest, leave the team, or are prone to burn out. Too much curiosity, on the other hand, leads to distractibility and inefficient behavior. It is up to the manager to read the context and synchronize curiosity and conformity. A good leader knows when to encourage the team to question things and when to move into action.

Back to Google.

The consequence, according to this new finding, is the opposite of what the Google research team was trying to prove. To put it in black and white: what the Google team came up with was it does not matter what caliber of people you put together, as long as you create the right conditions for them to flourish.

What are these conditions? They distilled five traits of effective teams, in the following order:

- Psychological safety: team members feel safe to take risks and can be vulnerable in front of each other.

- Dependability: team members collaboratively get things done on time and meet Google's high bar for excellence.

- Structure and clarity: team members have clear roles, plans, and goals for themselves and the collective.

- Meaning: work is personally important to team members.

- Impact: team members think their work matters and creates change.

The study revealed the team's greatest effectiveness boiled down to the environmental factors of the team rather than the attributes of its individual members. This research also sparked further research in this direction. The findings at Google were corroborated by the earlier research done by Anita Williams Woolley from Carnegie Mellon University and Christopher F. Chabris and Alex Pentland from MIT. These researchers found in 2010 that collective intelligence is not strongly correlated with the individual intelligence of group members. Putting together a bunch of smart people does not necessarily make the team smart as a system (Woolley 2010).

Woolley and her colleagues defined collective intelligence as the general ability of a group to perform a wide variety of old and new tasks. What they found is collective intelligence of a group is correlated with the average social sensitivity of group members (i.e., interpersonal empathy), the equality in distribution of conversational turn-taking (the ability of a team to let no one dominate the conversation but to invite everybody to speak up) and the proportion of women in the group (gender diversity) (Woolley 2010).

THE IMPORTANCE OF CONTEXT

Can we universalize this finding at Google to the rest of the corporate world? Does it hold true also for teams in totally different environments, such as high-stress environments or expeditions? Do we have to change our recruitment policies and instead of trying to find the best, hire just anybody? This is hard to believe.

Bill Gates is known to have confessed a good engineer is three hundred times more valuable for the organization than an average one. Surely, our intuition tells us individuals do matter. People, their individual energy, their drive, and their ideas do matter. This does not mean we should discredit the good work done at Google. They have uncovered an extra dimension. They have invited all of us to consider the other side of the coin, namely creating the right environment in the team is crucially important.

Sadly, this is something managers often forget. Continuously nurturing teams and providing them the right psychological safety, building on the diverse teams to pursue meaningful and stretched goals, and creating structure and clarity are all elements of what makes a successful and curious team.

In talking to Bill Fisher, professor of innovation and management at MIT Sloan, he shared context is a dimension we need to also take into consideration regarding teams. Some contexts require more nurture, some more nature. His opinion is the more extreme the situation, the more the individual aspects of the team members (and the leader) come into play. On the other hand, the less extreme the workplace, or the situation is normal, the more a nurturing environment is needed to create the right balance.

It is all about degrees. The team is a complex mix of both nature and nurture. Even though the percentages might be different depending on the situation, you need a combination of both. For Google, clearly the context across the 180 teams they researched was relatively equal, given they worked in the same company.

BENEFITS OF CURIOUS TEAMS

Team curiosity peaks when people are given a safe haven where they are appreciated for who they are, where their anxious thoughts and feelings are cared for by others, and where they have the opportunity to explore and speak up without fear.

Mike Pino, partner at PwC, shared a simple yet effective framework to describe the ideal mix of what people need in a team and thus what managers need to create. Probably coincidental, the abbreviation is his first name: "MIKE." People need:

1. Motivation

2. Incentives

3. Knowledge, skills, and abilities

4. Environment

He made a powerful analogy between management and gardening. "Having a fertile soil does not mean you will grow the fruit; you also need a good seed to begin with." In his own research, he had established the balance of these four dimensions will depend on the industry, the maturity of the team, the context, and the leadership style of the direct supervisor.

Teams with high curiosity levels are invariably supported by curious leaders. The impact on performance of less curious teams will be the opposite. I hope you prefer working for a curious team.

Curious teams perform better than incurious teams. They celebrate diversity, engage in open communication, and create a positively respectful, stimulating, and collaborative workplace atmosphere. The teams show an increased probability of functioning closer to optimality in the short and long term. This, in turn, leads to high performing teams where productivity, job satisfaction, engagement, and commitment are high. It is also a healthy contributor to workplace motivation and impacts attrition positively.

Curiosity reduces the conflict within the team. When a colleague takes a view of wondering why someone has a different opinion to her and explores in all openness what is behind her colleague's thinking, the dynamics between those two professionals will change from one of conflict into one of openness to listen and understand the other's point of view.

Curious teams display a greater willingness to try new things and see things from different perspectives. They experience less group conflict, given team members exhibit openness to each other and have proven to make fewer bad decisions because they are less influenced by groupthink.

DIFFERENT TEAMS CAN HAVE DIFFERENT CURIOSITY PROFILES

What I have discovered in my consulting across teams is customer facing teams are often stronger in their intellectual curiosity levels versus empathic or self-reflective curiosity. This curiosity about the world makes sense. They are driven by what happens to them daily. As a team, they are interested in and inquisitive about the external environment. Support teams, such as HR teams or shared services groups, tend to be more empathic as their primary skill. Also, this makes intuitive sense: their success is driven by the relationships they can establish with other teams in the organization.

This does not mean customer facing teams are not empathic; invariably, each team will have individuals who score strong on their empathic curiosity. Only in the customer-focusing teams I reviewed did their intellectual curiosity level tend to be higher.

When looking at self-reflective curiosity scores at an aggregate team level, most teams don't score particularly well. This insight is what teams often benefit most from. Once teams are presented with their team data, they suddenly realize they are high on intentional self-reflective curiosity. They don't take time to think, to do root cause analysis, to explore their collective biases, or to articulate their team values or team charters. In many teams, the habit of collective self-reflection is more prone to reactive behavior, and they are not aware of the group biases underpinning some of their decisions.

To prove this point, Nick van Dam, professor at IE University in Spain, shared another reason why curiosity is important for teams. He linked curiosity to the three sources for resistance in teams when reacting to a proposal for change. People have one of three reactions to a proposal for change.

1. They don't get it (and thus require more information, data, or insights).

2. They don't like it.

3. They don't like you.

According to Professor van Dam, the level of openness of the individual team members as well as the collective openness toward each other are important factors in creating a change-inviting environment. Building on this, my research has found if people feel they can be genuinely curious at work, this has a direct correlation to their readiness to accept organizational change. When working in a curious team, people are more easily able to ask how change can work for them.

When people find themselves in an incurious environment, they will often also react incuriously. In the face of change, they respond with anxiety, less exploration, change resistance, and preference of the status quo. Incurious teams usually react negatively to change. Curious teams respond proactively to change. They listen, ask questions, digest data, and then respond.

THE NINE DIMENSIONS OF CURIOUS TEAMS

The date—a late spring afternoon on June 17, 2021. After eighteen months of COVID-19 isolation, Patrick van Erp and Jack Vroomen decided to get their entire company together for team building in a picturesque tavern of the beautiful city of Sittard in the Southern Netherlands. The loosening of the lockdown regulations allowed more people to meet again physically after many marathons of videoconferences. It was a relief and a joy to see each other face to face. What might have been even more exciting was the overarching theme of the workshop: workplace curiosity. The two owners of the thirty-member-strong management consulting company Ponthus had been preparing for the next stage in the company's development and were preparing to test the waters for their big plans with the team.

Since starting Ponthus about ten years ago, Patrick and Jack made sure to create a healthy balance between exploitation and exploration in their company. Exploitation was all about putting their resources at the service of their clients and creating sustainable change for them. Exploration was the other side of the coin. Every employee has 25 percent of her time available to focus on learning and experimentation. It's important to Patrick and Jack to create this friendly atmosphere receptive to curiosity, while at the same time, instilling a work hard combined with its counterbalance, "play hard."

Every month, prior to COVID-19, on a Friday afternoon between 4:00 and 5:00 p.m., the entire team would gather together in a room above their favorite local bar in Sittard with the only agenda point of knowledge sharing, followed by a glass of beer or soda downstairs. Another aspect of the family feeling is transparency. Every quarter, the entire team came together to review the financials of the company, discuss current and new clients, and get up to date on the latest thinking of the owners. Transparency also means everybody is invited to speak up and be heard during these sessions.

A profitable business, solid customer contracts, new product diversification and capital investments, and the desire to capitalize on the COVID-19 experience created the right cocktail for a positive impetus in the company. While they were getting ready to start hiring new people in the company, Patrick and Jack wanted to bring the entire team together around the original cultural tenets the company was built upon, namely customer excellence, growth, and family. As with so many companies, COVID-19 had been destabilizing for them and the founders wanted to make sure these values remained top of mind for all. They had become aware a new injection of energy was needed to get ideas flowing again post-COVID-19.

When reflecting on the past, present, and future, both realized new ideas were needed from all and it needed to be structured even more intentionally. For instance, the owners agreed the age difference between them, and their team was dampening idea flows. This needed to be tackled.

"Though my office is always open, people are not queuing up with new ideas all the time. If we want to grow, we need to take a step back so we can jump ever further, and that's why we decided to bring in the focus on curiosity in the team," said van Erp.

During their analysis, we mapped their organizational curiosity culture. This diagnostic is customer designed by building on the latest research on workplace curiosity, individual curiosity, organizational success, and high performing teams. It consists of nine dimensions: manager relations and style, learning culture, diversity of curious individuals, curiosity processes and practices, culture of openness, psychological safety, the availability of role models, vision clarity, and innovation orientation/failure acceptance. The advantage of the diagnostic is it can compare organizations, even intact teams within the same organization.

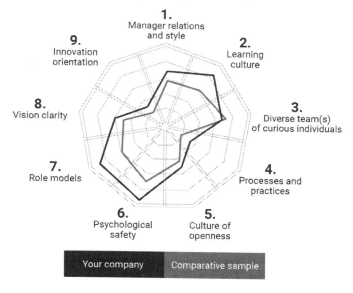

The Nine Dimensions of Curious Teams: Ponthus Case

Your company compared to peers

1. Manager relations and style
2. Learning culture
3. Diverse team(s) of curious individuals
4. Processes and practices
5. Culture of openness
6. Psychological safety
7. Role models
8. Vision clarity
9. Innovation orientation

Your company | Comparative sample

The results for Ponthus were an indication the company was doing well in virtually all dimensions as compared to other companies in the database. This did, however, not mean Patrick and Jack could rest on their laurels. While they were good at psychological safety, role models, and learning culture, some areas like innovation orientation, processes and practices, and culture of openness were areas the team felt it could do better.

The explanation of the nine dimensions of curious teams can be understood as follows:

1. Manager relations and style: A supporting leader encouraging and enabling the team to be curious.

2. Learning culture: Opportunities and time for individuals to grow and learn.

3. Diverse team of curious individuals: Gender diversity in a team of highly curious individuals.

4. Curiosity-enabling processes and practices: Underlying processes enabling the sustainability of workplace curiosity.

5. Culture of openness: Openness to ideas and questions, including their activation through exploration.

6. Psychological safety: A conducive climate where every member can show up, contribute, and take risks.

7. Role models: The availability for curious role models at all levels.

8. Vision clarity: The ambient team and organizational clarity provided by a clear strategy propelling focused action.

9. Innovation orientation: Readiness to explore and implement innovation as well as acceptance of mistakes in the pursuit of excellence.

During the highly interactive workshop, the team worked hard on both understanding their curiosity through the lens of curiosity and, at the same time, attempting a bottom-up formulation of areas that could make the team better.

Here are some of those improvement suggestions:

- Create organic curiosity teams: informal teams who cook up something new for the company.

- Appoint the tenth person, i.e., appoint a challenger person in meetings whose only task it is to make the group focus on the right discussion.

- Introduce innovation days and show off innovation we are working on with each other and customers.

- Create monthly inspiration sessions within the entire team, e.g., lunch and learn sessions where the topic also could be where we are not doing well.

- Create a mental model and template to combine both depth and breadth in learning.

- Short-term internships with IT suppliers and customers.

- Make some changes to the office.

- Share compliments/personal things.

- Create product/industry teams to deepen knowledge in both as a team.

- Ask owners to share even more about their vision and where they wanted to take the company.

- Profile Ponthus even more as a hub of information and leverage the ecosystem.

- Engage in curiosity diagnostics and awareness workshops with customers.

- Do more job rotation across teams.

Is an organization nothing more than a team of teams, or is an organization more than the sum of its teams? As we have already touched upon in our nine dimensions model, there are organizational dimensions which can be tackled at the organizational level. I am referring especially to those areas such as (curiosity-enabling) processes and practices, the level of openness and dialogue the senior leadership invites, the overall strategy it pursues, and the overall level of innovation orientation. Let's look at curious organizations now.

WHAT CAN TEAMS DO TO GET BETTER AT TEAM CURIOSITY?

The strategies I suggest here are meant as a collective reflection moment in the team. If you want to explore improvement strategies more. I suggest you visit the chapter on architecting curiosity to get (even) better at curiosity later in this book.

- Measure curiosity: baseline and create measurements.

- Create exploration meetings: no-agenda meetings.

- Introduce the team to tools to enhance their collective curiosity muscle.

- Embrace psychological safety.

- Create the right level of diversity.

- Discover, explore, and discuss team values.

The Big Ideas

Team curiosity is more than just the sum of the curiosity of the individuals, and collective intelligence is not the same as the sum of individual intelligence. Curious individuals need curious environments—and curious teams—to thrive. High-performing teams are curious teams, teams where both individuals show up curiously and where the environment intentionally creates the right extra conditions.

There are clear benefits to unleashing curiosity in a team. Curious teams are more likely to celebrate diversity, engage in open communication, and create a positively respectful, stimulating, and collaborative workplace atmosphere. Such teams show an increased probability of functioning closer to optimality in the short and long term. This, in turn, leads to productive teams where job satisfaction, motivation engagement, and commitment are high and where attrition is low.

The leader has a big responsibility in creating the right balance between efficiency and curiosity, between exploitation and exploration. Excellent leaders know when they need to allow curiosity and when agile implementation is called for.

Team curiosity can be measured and baselined for the team. The nine-dimensional model is a good way to analyze the current state and guide the team toward a collective action plan.

Questions for Reflection

- How diverse is the team composition in your group?

- When a new member joins the team, how seamlessly does the team welcome the new team member?

- How do you align you team? Are the team values articulated and understood by all team members?

- On which side of the curiosity-conformity scale would you say your team is? (Tip: The ideal place is in the middle.)

- What are the strengths of the team when looking through the lens of curiosity?

8

ORGANIZATIONS: CURIOSITY AT SCALE

―――

"A growth mindset thrives in the diversity of ideas and if the culture inhibits psychological safety, then people may not freely bring both good and bad ideas forward, which will limit innovation."

—SATYA NADELLA, CEO, MICROSOFT

How different are teams from organizations, other than size and numbers of people? Does curiosity work the same way whether you are talking about a small group or a large group?

GROWTH MINDSET IN ACTION

I have always been intrigued by how the culture and values of an organization can show up differently in different offices. For instance, in global organizations, if you visit different regional offices, say London, Beijing, and Mexico City offices, you find yourself in a different atmosphere.

Such different atmospheres are found also across teams. The design team will invariably have a different feel than the legal team. It depends on the context they work in, the kind of people who work there, the average age, the management style, the local culture, and many other dimensions. Focusing on the nuclear unit of the team to drive organizational success is the right strategy. Curiosity is felt at the level of the team.

This does not mean the overarching organization, or the C-suite, has no role to play. Quite the contrary. Though it is possible to find pockets of curious teams in otherwise incurious environments, the culture and climate the CEO creates has a direct impact on the curiosity level of the organization.

At an organizational level, curiosity is the driver for creativity and innovation. When comparing curiosity to the growth mindset concept, I agree with curiosity researcher and leadership consultant Alison Horstmeyer:

"Curiosity is growth mindset in action."

Curiosity does not settle for the status quo; instead, it retains a healthy level of humility and allows divergent opinions to emerge. It also supports organizational learning through active openness to processes, like after-action reviews, especially a desire to learn from things that went south. Curious organizations create a positive brand for themselves. When I ask people about their top three curious companies, Steve Jobs' Apple is often mentioned. Most people want to work for successful brands with a clearly articulated purpose.

Curious organizations allow for curiosity to thrive through their culture, processes, and practices and believe the curiosity muscle of every employee needs to be nourished. They also believe this muscle can be enhanced with curiosity-enhancing tools to unlock its power. They know to tap into the collective wisdom of all employees they need to embrace curiosity and banish fear. As John Hunt in *The Art of The Idea* writes, "Fear might be a strong catalyst for entrenching obedience, but it's a lousy motivator for fresh thinking" (Hunt 2009).

Though the C-suite and management in organizations are generally in favor of the notion of curiosity, the situation on the ground can be different.

MICROSOFT

Did Satya Nadella fully know he was about to start an internal revolution at Microsoft when he took the helm in February 2014? He did realize, under his predecessor Steve Ballmer, Microsoft had become a sluggish multinational company. Steve Ballmer had grown the business, yet he had steered Microsoft in an unfavorable direction. While the first stint of Microsoft under Bill Gates can be characterized as entrepreneurial, CEO Ballmer had introduced a reductive textbook management culture. Conformity and obedience were more important than curiosity and challenging the status quo. People in power, whether they were technical experts or in leadership positions, were carrying weight and not to be questioned. They also were supposed to have unwavering answers to all questions, or so they told themselves.

Satya Nadella realized brewing underneath was an unhealthy culture. Instead of focusing on the easy way out, i.e., organizational restructuring and lay-offs, his surgery tackled something deeper: the underlying culture. Before he tackled his partnership strategy, acquisitions, and technology investments, he refocused the company toward a growth mindset, curiosity, and non-violent conversations. What is important to know is this mindset was already part of his own personality, and he was able to imprint his beliefs and values on this organization. In Mr. Nadella's own words, "A growth mindset thrives in the diversity of ideas, and if the culture inhibits psychological safety, then people may not freely bring both good and bad ideas forward, which will limit innovation" (Hoffman 2021).

The results of the Microsoft turnaround are remarkable.

Beyond early start-ups, which often have a highly curious and passionate founder, I am seeing other companies also embracing curiosity for their organizations. For instance, the CEO of Novartis, Vas Narasimhan, is also a highly curious individual: he has imprinted his personality on Novartis by changing its people values to "inspired, unbossed, and curious"—this has led the HR team to change their processes and their L&D organization to focus more on curiosity. It starts most of the time at the top, yet it does not have to be this way. I have observed single teams create the right curious environment for themselves before the wider organization got interested.

What we have seen is since the end of the twentieth century and the recent COVID-19 crisis, change can be difficult for those companies not open to it. We can easily remember IBM believing a PC in every home would be foolish, Kodak not envisioning digital photography would take over analog photography, or Nokia not believing phones would be smarter than just talking voice devices. Even if some of their employees saw the storm coming, most of them did not, or at least the collective mind of these organizations did not give space to these new ideas to flourish.

During COVID-19, we have seen in the same industries, some companies are thriving while others are barely surviving. This is because they are allowing for curiosity. They retain a level of wonder of what could be, a level of humility to make sure they don't become arrogant, and a level of openness to make them change.

Curious organizations are organizations engaging in two activities above what other successful companies do. First, they are intentional about creating the right environment for curiosity to flourish through their culture, values, processes, and practices. Second, they are also intentional about helping those individuals, leaders, and teams in building a curious mindset. Simply instructing people to "just be curious" does not make them so.

CURIOSITY AS THE NORTH STAR

Some companies have curiosity in their corporate values and are using this value as a North Star to follow. This is remarkable. When sharing a list of thirty companies on LinkedIn with curiosity articulated in their values, I got different reactions. Some people were proud of their organizations, yet some others were hesitant. When talking to them, some of them confessed curiosity is the most difficult value they have, or it is the least developed one. One company executive shared with me that curiosity referred to the original work ethic of the company's founders, yet their entrepreneurial (and curious) spirit had long been replaced by risk-averse management structures. A third type of reply to my post came from start-ups for not being included in the list, yet who had curiosity articulated in their values.

Start-ups are a good breeding ground for curiosity.

Organizational curiosity, just like individual curiosity, is a muscle that must be developed. Workplace curiosity in multinational companies can be a force to increase competitiveness, innovation, productivity, learning, and engagement, yet it is fragile if not managed intentionally. Even when they are not proactively engaged in curiosity, most organizations do have the foundations to build curious cultures. Harvard professor Francesca Gino confirmed, "By making small changes to the design of their organization and the ways they manage employees, leaders can encourage curiosity and improve their companies and make rapid changes" (Gino 2018).

Before we dive in further, it is important to state the obvious: curiosity is not a free for all. The best organizations and leaders can know when to allow for exploration and when to stop exploration and move into exploitation. Agility and curiosity go hand in hand. In December 2020, the company SurveyMonkey came out with a report stating, the combined set of curiosity and agility were the two best predictors whether a company would survive the backlash of COVID-19. They defined curiosity as the openness to try new things and agility as the speed by which these new things could be productized or materialized. This also has been my finding in the context of effective curious leaders. Curious leaders know when to allow curiosity/ ideation/experimentation and when to move to action (SurveyMonkey 2020).

Another way to look at this is the following: Agility means the ability to change fast and be flexible. Curiosity is the underlying mindset as it provides the desire to change and provides its overall direction. Interestingly, both agility and curiosity are relatively new concepts in the management literature.

INTENTIONALITY VERSUS THE CHERNOBYL EFFECT

The Chernobyl nuclear power plant disaster is an extreme example of how things can go wrong. According to the online *Encyclopedia Britannica*, the reason the core of the nuclear power plant in Ukraine melted was one of a series of human errors that could have been avoided. It is a telling metaphor for companies and incuriosity, a closed, fixed, and conformist mindset, and a collective cognitive bias. It shows a disregard for broader exploration of the reasons behind a crisis and a desire to ask only questions when the answers are predictable.

Curiosity is not reserved only for start-ups. I have observed scale-ups and large organizations who are also able to embrace the notion of exploration as part of their operations; who are creating cultures, processes, and practices to celebrate curiosity, who allow their employees to take calculated risks and encourage them to stick out their necks; who create a climate of openness where it is okay to ask questions, and it is not a blemish if the leader does not have all the answers. Curious organizations also have learned, it is more profitable to treat people like creative authentic agents rather than cogs in a mechanistic system, able to be exchanged at a whim.

Intentionality is an important factor in management. If left to chance, curiosity will likely not flourish. What gets measured gets done. Some companies are intentional about workplace curiosity in a single process (e.g., curiosity only reserved for leadership) or single function (e.g., curiosity only valued in departments such as R&D or HR functions such as recruitment or learning and development).

WHO WOULD YOU PROMOTE?

No company is 100 percent curious or 100 percent incurious. There are gradations of curiosity as well as levels of intentionality. All companies are to be found somewhere between these two extremes. Indeed, organizational curiosity is a state. It is something that evolves, something that grows or withers. Start-ups tend to be high on curiosity. One dimension of curiosity is the acceptance of failure: in comparing start-ups with global large-scale traditional organizations, I have found start-ups are four times readier to learn from failures versus established organizations. This also means large organizations are four times less ready to consider failures as learning opportunities.

Curiosity is the driver for innovation, for never settling for the status quo, for retaining a healthy level of organizational humility, for actively allowing divergent opinions to emerge. It also supports organizational learning through active openness to processes like for instance after-action-reviews, especially a desire to learn from things that went south.

Though the C-suite and management in organizations are generally in favor of the notion of curiosity the situation on the ground can be different. When asking professionals whether their organizations are curious, about 84 percent are positive. This makes sense; we can all associate some form of curiosity on the work floor. Seventy-four percent of the same group of professionals, however, also share their organizations created barriers that stifle curiosity.

These findings are echoed by research from Harvard Business School studying curiosity from employees in a wide range of firms and industries. The researchers found only about 24 percent reported feeling curious in their jobs on a regular basis, and about 70 percent said they face barriers to asking more questions at work (Gino 2018).

Organizations can support or stifle curiosity through its practices, processes, culture, and climate. I often present the following situation to executives. Imagine you are part of a promotion committee. Your brief is to review the cases of two candidates and select only one of them to be promoted.

1. Jeff deserves to be on the list. He performed consistently over time and has proven year after year to be a loyal employee. Whatever challenges he is asked to take on, he will deliver. Managers like him.

2. Mary also has made it to the shortlist. She also has been performing well in her core tasks. Some colleagues have complained she does not always follow the rules. She is known to ask tough questions of management. She has been fiercely loyal. Last year, she volunteered to join a team looking at an innovative customer project. If successful, this project would have the potential of bigger things. Even the board was interested in this project. As it happens, the project failed miserably. Nobody dares to talk about it.

Who will you promote?

I have done this experiment with thousands of people. What I find time after time is: executives say their organizations promote Jeff; while at the same time they add, it should be in fact Mary who should be promoted.

TRAITS OF CURIOUS COMPANIES

We can distill the following differences between curious and incurious companies.

Comparing traits of curious versus incurious companies

INCURIOUS COMPANIES	CURIOUS COMPANIES
Suffer from collective cognitive bias	Are aware of their biases, encourage openness, and see first time failures as an opportunity to learn
Disregard the evolving environment and new entrants	Have deep interest in the evolving landscape and how the company can adapt
Focus on the known world	Focus both on improving their current processes as well as actively exploring adjacent and new opportunities
Adhere to efficiency strategies based on historic expertise	Have a dual focus: exploration and exploitation
Accept managerial arrogance	Promote confident humility
Focus only on efficiency objectives at the expense of openness to change	Adopt key performance indicators to focus both on efficiency of current initiatives as well as new innovations
Think curiosity is distracting from its focus and is at best linked to continuous improvement	Believe curiosity is part of the corporate culture which needs to be embedded across the organisation
Examples: Kodak, Microsoft pre-2014, Nokia, Blockbuster	*Examples: Netflix, Microsoft post-2014, Novartis, McKinsey & Company*

Curious companies see first-time failures as an opportunity to learn. They have a clarity of vision and strategy. They are driven by an intentional curious culture and create the right processes and practices to support both exploration and exploitation. In such companies, we find high levels of psychological safety and diversity of gender, thought, and experience.

OBLIGATION TO DISSENT

Do you support employees in your companies who dissent?

In my interview with Dr. Nick van Dam, former chief learning officer and partner at McKinsey & Company and now professor and human development scientist at IE university in Madrid, he immediately started talking about his experience at McKinsey when I asked him for his opinion about archetypes of curious organizations.

One of the values held high in the company is its obligation to dissent, he shared. Every employee, from the day they join the company, is asked to dissent where they think they should. This means not only being told it is okay to disagree, even stronger: it is expected. There is a realization older and more experienced people do not have all the knowledge and new perspectives are welcomed and rewarded, not punished.

I have also experienced this type of behavior firsthand as a customer of McKinsey & Company. All McKinsey consultants I worked with on strategy projects showed up as smart, data-driven consultants with a strong initial listening bias as they wanted to understand my corporate landscape as quickly as possible. Once they were up to speed, they became co-creators of the new processes, not as merely translators of my management team's and my own points of view, but also with a clear license to dissent in case they felt our approaches were not deeply thought through or not data-driven enough if present operations started to dictate the narrative. This was clearly a strength I admired and welcomed.

McKinsey consultants I worked with shared some of their internal practices with me, practices that ensure the intellectual curiosity of their consultants is kept high. For instance, consultants need to keep their knowledge proactively up to date and share their growth. To support this, McKinsey has automated the individual online profiles of each consultant in the company: every time a consultant (co)writes a paper, takes a course, or works on a customer project, the individual profile gets automatically updated. "About 90 percent of the content on each consultant's internal profile gets populated automatically, 10 percent can be added manually," they shared, "This creates positive stress among consultants to keep constantly building and sharing knowledge."

They further confirmed with me, "The better one's CV, the easier one gets invited to new and interesting projects and the better it is for internal promotion. What we write gets appreciated internally, yet even more so if it gets published in *McKinsey Quarterly* or other external platforms. Also joining courses to up-skill oneself instead of being billed on customer projects is expected of all."

McKinsey also over-indexes on other processes to create a curious culture supporting curious minds. From the time consultants join the company, they are encouraged to "make your own McKinsey," meaning they are empowered to create their own career path. Not a predetermined top-down path the manager, human resources, or the organization forces upon people, but a path everyone creates for her or himself.

McKinsey is particularly good at its onboarding process. Van Dam particularly mentioned the new manager onboarding program in this regard.

"Becoming a team manager is a big thing at McKinsey. If you are part of the select few invited to become a manager, one typically has spent about six years with the company, has proved to be good in an individual contributor consulting role, and has shown leadership qualities in line with McKinsey's values."

To support these new managers, they are invited to join the INSPIRE program, which is a week-long program in one of the leadership centers of McKinsey.

During these five days secluded in the mountains, managers don't focus on the operational aspects of being a good people manager, but instead are invited to reflect on their own individual purpose, value system, and beliefs. "This is a powerful experience, and sometimes so powerful that people decide to leave the company at the end of this program if they realize after deep self-reflection that their career path is elsewhere."

A powerful side note is McKinsey does not think ill of these people who resign but embraces them as alumni and keeps nourishing the relationship with them post departure. This is not only driven by empathy, but McKinsey alumni also tend to end up in senior corporate roles and once in need of consulting power, they often invite McKinsey to do the work.

What we learn from this, is McKinsey & Company is an example of an above average curious global company. One could be easily sidetracked by the fact this strategic consulting company is so particular, it cannot provide lessons for other companies.

I beg to differ: a culture of obligation to dissent, a proactive job rotation, a thorough recruitment process, focus on helping new managerial talent to explore themselves first to ground them more as a prelude to managing others, empowering employees to chart their own career journey are all dimensions other companies can learn from…. Surely it is not easy to copy such practices, yet with the right intent, discipline, and focus, it can make a difference toward becoming a curious organization.

CURIOUS MINDS DEDICATED TO HUMAN PROGRESS

When it comes to curiosity, Merck KGaA, Darmstadt, Germany is one of the more intentional companies I have had the good fortune to study. They are intentional about curiosity. They actively measure and steer curiosity, they sponsor academic research about curiosity, they enable curiosity in both of their processes (e.g., recruitment, product innovation, training), and they also train people and teams on practical ways to engage more with their own curiosity mindset.

Christine Blum-Heuser, associate director of the company's brand initiative and involved in its curiosity initiative since 2015, shared with me a fundamental belief they share within the company: "Innovative thinking can come from anybody and anywhere, inside and outside the organization, from all levels, not only the experts."

As early as 2015, the company began adopting intentional curiosity. Initially, it was a theme combining the deeper nature of their three distinct businesses, i.e., pharma, life sciences, and electronics. Quickly, it became a global initiative encompassing their entire organization. They have been working with academics to look for ways to measure, influence, and foster curiosity at levels of the individual, team, and organization. They train their employees on topics such as stress management (the biggest detractor of curiosity), innovative question strategies, training to explore alternative strategies, and hypothesis testing to mention a few.

Curiosity has also been embraced in the recruitment branding promise of Merck KGaA, Darmstadt, Germany to new employees with this statement: "Bring your curiosity to life."

That curiosity is not merely a nice-to-have for the company is highlighted by Christine.

> Curiosity plays a major role in creating flexibility of thinking of our employees and their willingness to leave the beaten path and pioneer new directions. It's not about methods we use per se; it is more about the mindset at individual, team, and organizational level. If we fail to be curious, we lose potential and positive opportunities.

When asking her what lessons she has learned that could be relevant for other companies, she listed the following:

- Become aware of the deeper impact curiosity can play in your organization.

- Excite people. Curiosity is a sleeping beauty. People often bring their curiosity to life in their private lives; you need to welcome it into the workplace and trigger it.

- Have an executive sponsor. Enable from the top and create the right structure and organizational desire.

- Enable from the bottom. Create a pull factor. Make your employees want to join you in your curiosity journey. Enable them with curiosity mindset training.

- Make it a company value. Embed curiosity in your underlying value system.

Remember, curiosity is something we're born with, or the spark that kickstarted your company. We just need to find our way back to looking at the world and asking, "Why?" and "How?" and "What's possible?" Imagine what our organizations could achieve when people begin learning and asking questions about the things they want to know about. When they do, new strategies emerge.

The strategy process is the focus of the next chapter. At an aggregated level, how do the CEO and his team create a supporting strategy enabling them to fully embrace the past, the present, and the future? Easier said than done, we will see the strategy process in companies is often a difficult dance between continuing the status quo and exploring new horizons.

The Big Idea

Workplace curiosity is a force to increase competitiveness, innovation, productivity, learning, and engagement, yet it is fragile if not managed intentionally. By making small changes to the design of their organizations and the way they manage their employees, leaders can encourage curiosity.

In the light of accelerated economic activity toward the fourth industrial revolution driven by infotech and biotech, companies cannot afford to be incurious. An incurious organization will become complacent, will not learn from mistakes, will be arrogant, and will miss the corner of innovation in the light of new competition.

Workplace curiosity can be a force to increase competitiveness, innovation, productivity, learning, and engagement, yet is fragile if not managed intentionally.

Curiosity is best expressed at the level of the team, yet top leadership has a huge influence in how they shape the culture and influence processes and practices of their organization.

By making small changes to the design of their organizations and the ways they manage their employees, leaders can encourage curiosity and improve their companies. This is true in every industry and for creative and routine work alike. Every company has the right foundation to build on. Organizational curiosity is not reserved for start-ups or for new age enterprises.

Many organizations have embedded curiosity in their corporate values and strategic charters. These companies are helping others in making the case for change.

Questions for Reflection

- If you were asked to advise your CEO or your board to make changes to embrace workplace curiosity even more, what single advice would you give them?

- When considering your corporate culture, would you say your company errs on the side of curiosity or more on the side of conformity? (Tip: The objective of the company is to be good at both.)

- What best practices can you think of excellence in curiosity in your company or in other companies?

- How widely accepted is failure? Is it celebrated as a learning opportunity, or is it a career-limiting move?

- How easy is it to innovate at your level, suggest improvements, and implement them?

PART THREE

THE CURIOSITY ENABLERS

9

CURIOSITY'S ROLE IN CORPORATE STRATEGY

———

"When we are curious, we are better able to look at stress as something we can enhance our performance rather than finding it to be paralyzing."
—FRANCESCA GINO, BEHAVIORAL SCIENTIST,
HARVARD BUSINESS SCHOOL

Xie Gelan knew she could not celebrate New Year's Eve with her family. She was a computer support engineer for Nokia in Beijing, China. For over a year, she—frankly, all people involved in computers globally—faced a conundrum. Will the wheels of the world stop spinning when the clocks chime midnight on the evening of December 31, 1999? The scenario was real in the head of Xie Gelan, yet, like all her peers, she did not have an answer. What would happen to all computers in the world when the year in the internal computer chips would move from 1999 to 2000?

Worst case scenario was airplanes would fall out of the sky. For a telecom company like Nokia, telephone communication just might stop functioning all together. She was curious, not the type of curiosity she had experienced with her newborn, but a curiosity driven by anxiety, like when she waited for the results of her uncle's cancer test. The challenge to be solved was called "the millennium bug" or the "Y2K" bug among specialists like Xie Gelan.

Luckily for Xie Gelan and all of us, nothing happened that night. It was the sentiment with which we all started the twenty-first century. It was an accelerated way to shed our twentieth century skin. It started with a digital crisis on the eve of the twenty-first century with a scenario where the digital engine of the world would stop because of Y2K. The hysteria projected computers would reset themselves and lose all worldwide data the moment the clock turned from 1999 into 2000. While many people were partying at the millennium crossover, IT professionals and leaders around the world were praying the damage would be containable. Nothing happened, yet the tone was set. The twenty-first century was going to be different.

Different it has been indeed. Several companies have started to call out curiosity as a key ingredient for their strategy and continued growth—Microsoft, Novartis, 3M, and Google to name a few of the bigger players. About thirty of such large companies have included curiosity as an overarching corporate value. Many smaller organizations have adopted curiosity as an intentional way of doing business.

I have always been interested in exploring the underlying reason why we do things the way we do. When reasoning about the origins of our current approach to management, Frederick Taylor is probably the most towering management thinker of the twentieth century as he laid the foundations upon which current companies are built. He founded scientific management and introduced the concepts of efficient production processes, which culminated in concepts such as total quality management and the LEAN and Six Sigma movements. He even introduced the concept of organization charts. Without him, the corporate world we live in would likely look very different.

FREDERICK TAYLOR AND SCIENTIFIC MANAGEMENT

Twenty-five hundred years ago, Aristotle realized harmony in the middle was better than going for extremes.

Why is it then the prevalent management theory that was—and often still is—taught at MBA schools is one of focusing on only one extreme, namely on exploitation at the expense of exploration? We need to start embracing both. The challenge of doing both is so difficult because they are grounded in fundamentally different mental models. Being good in one does not automatically mean you are good in both.

Exploitation versus Exploration

	EXPLOITATION (20th CENTURY SKILL)	EXPLORATION (21th CENTURY SKILL)
EMPHASIS ON	Old certainties	New possibilities
INTENDED OUTCOME	Getting results	Building potential
ACHIEVING CONTINUITY THROUGH	Stability	Renewal
VALUE CREATION THROUGH	Efficiency & effectiveness	Rejuvenation & innovation
DOMINANT MIND-SET	Stay focused	Keep openminded
LEADERSHIP PRIORITY	Offering clarity	Offering new opportunities
PREFERRED STRATEGY TOOLS	Planning & control cycles	Innovation pipelines & markets
COMMON RISK	Stability leads to stagnation	Renewal leads to chaos

Source: Adapted from Meyer and Meyers (2013)

Most large and small companies have adopted Taylorism as a management methodology, one with a single focus on exploitation and one where exploration is frowned upon. In times of stability, this is a perfectly appropriate strategy. In times of disruption and change, however, blocking innovation and new ideas and using the past

as a yardstick for the future leads to stagnation and ultimately demise.

From the 1920s onward, companies were quick to adopt Taylor's thinking. The dominating mindset of enterprises became
one of ensuring stability and continuity, which meant a focus
on maintaining the status quo rather than innovation. The
focus was on looking backward rather than forward. History
was the best guide to predict the future, agree on budget,
and plan projects. Old certainties were more important than
new opportunities. Preferred strategy tools were planning
and control cycles, and value was created through doubling
down on efficiency and effectiveness. There is nothing wrong
with this model. It was the best possible way to manage the
industrial landscape throughout the twentieth century.

In this model, people are divided into thinkers and doers in organizations. Like in the army, thinking is the prerogative of people in
power; everybody else is supposed to implement the directives of
their leaders. Thinking outside the box or suggesting new ideas is
not expected, it is even discouraged. Even managers are penalized
if they delegate too much to their teams. Senior management sets
the strategy and makes the decisions, mid management oversees
its implementation, and frontline management takes care of the
day-to-day operations under a watchful eye of the executives
above. The paradigm of workers is one of resources, albeit more
unpredictable resources than financial or material resources. In
this model, workers cannot be trusted too much on their own but
need constant supervision and must be told what to do.

Fear is thought to be the underlying motivator to manage the
troops. The underlying assumption is people who are afraid

(of being ostracized, of their bosses, or of potential rewards) will work hard, and as a result, good things will happen for the organization.

Nowadays, we know fear inhibits curiosity, which in turn negatively impacts learning, cooperation, and innovation. In such a system, being safe and keeping ideas to oneself is often better than to volunteer them and be sorry afterward.

In a system focused on efficiency, mistakes are viewed as something that should be avoided at all costs.

HUBBLE VERSUS CHALLENGER

Kurt Verweire, strategy professor at the Vlerick Business School in Belgium, advocates an ambidextrous approach to strategy: one celebrating both exploitation of the past and present as well as exploration of the future. The challenge he has observed in working with leadership teams is this is often too conceptual and difficult for most leaders to operationalize.

In his research and work with executive teams, he has found two approaches to innovation, both which need curiosity. The most prevalent approach to innovation is where innovation is happening outside the core of the organization, where innovation is happening in a ring-fenced part of the organization. Supported directly by the CEO or a senior leader, the new business is often managed by a natural explorer, the type of driven leader who is not afraid to break some eggshells. Professor Verweire coins this model the "Hubble" model, referring to the Hubble telescope that observes the universe while being in space itself. Innovation is disruptive here.

On the other hand, Professor Verweire shared another—though less disruptive—approach less written about in the strategy literature: the change from within. He described transformations from inside the existing core of the organization or business group. Often being launched as a small change initiative within the business, the initial pilot contaminates its environment and creates change across the business. He refers to this model as the "Challenger" model an analogy to the NASA spacecrafts that depart from Houston and return after every flight. Innovation serves both disruption as well as continuous improvement, yet, in most cases, is more related to continuous or evolutionary change.

Companies need to be both on the lookout for disruption in unlikely places beyond their industry and on top of continuously improving their products and services for the following reason. New entrants, devoid of tradition, can see beyond the familiar world of the incumbents. They are faster to come up with radical new approaches and business models. Think about how Airbnb is transforming the hospitality business, or how Uber is transforming the mobility business.

No industries are safe; even Google is entering the healthcare market. Eastman Kodak was not able to face the onslaught of the digital photography era. It is proving harder for companies to go beyond the known world and explore a different universe they were not part of. This is a function of the difference between organizational narrow and broad curiosity we discussed earlier. Narrow curiosity leads to continuous improvement; broad organizational curiosity leads to radically new disruptions.

An important point Professor Verweire made was the commonly held notion exploitation is for "managers" and exploration for "leaders." In his own words, "this would mean exploitation is easy, can be done by anybody, and can even be outsourced. Ambidexterity actually requires deep skills in both." He agrees, in many organizations, there is an inbuilt preference to emphasize exploitation at the expense of exploration.

Exploitation is predictable, can be measured, leads directly to the bottom line, and is in the present. Exploration, on the other hand, is uncertain, harder to measure, is an investment, and is only relevant in the future. Exploration might also distract the team from their efficiency focus.

This comment that exploitation and exploration are both important resonates with the research by the INSEAD researcher Spencer Harrison. He found in his research into curiosity as it relates to the C-level in organizations if CEOs and their executive teams are high in productive workplace curiosity, their organization is better at both exploitation as well as exploration. This is an important finding. Especially as managerial curiosity can be linked also to an improved exploitation mindset. Curiosity clearly does not only favor the explorers (Harrison 2021).

JUMPING S-CURVES

The need for curiosity shows itself not in times when things are going well, but in crisis. A good metaphor to describe this analogy is with the concept of S-curves. This concept shows innovation follows the shape of the letter "S" (Nunes 2011).

S-curve

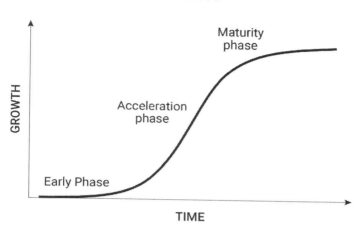

S Curve Graph

Early on, growth and returns are flat. As technology or process matures, the organization experiences an acceleration phase (a steeper line). Finally, the product or service stabilizes over time, resulting in another flattening of the line. All products and services follow this structure. Depending on several dimensions (such as complexity of the offering, competitive landscape, etc.), the time it takes between the launch, maturity, and decline of the product or services can range between decades and months. The S-curve for Kodak's analogue film business was almost a century old and long. The S-curve for software applications can be only several months before a better version is introduced in the market.

When the environment changes, companies need to reinvent themselves to face the new realities. In the language of the S-curve, they need to jump to a new S-curve and start the process again.

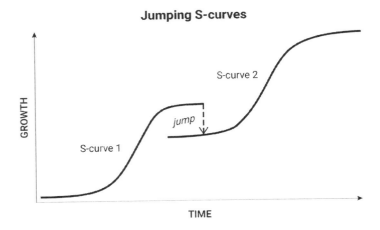

Jumping S-curves

GROWTH

S-curve 2

jump

S-curve 1

TIME

If we make the connection to curiosity, we can observe curiosity helps in optimizing the S-curve, yet even more so creates the right conditions to help jump the organization to the next S-curve. Kodak was not able to jump from their successful S-curve of analogue photography to the next S-curve, which represented digital photography.

Microsoft also had difficulty in jumping S-curves when Steve Ballmer took over. In early 2000, Bill Gates handed over the CEO position to Steve Ballmer. Within a year, Microsoft's market cap dropped in half and the employees' stock options were essentially worthless. Microsoft was not alone as the dot-com crash had affected most companies. Ballmer was then facing a new reality Gates never had to experience: a company suddenly struggling and needing to reinvent itself. The way he went about this transformation led to the creation of a lesser version of itself, one where Microsoft the company could not face the challenges in the market as it used to do.

Ballmer inherited the most valuable company in the world, one whose success relied on a near monopoly of desktop computers running on MS Windows, MS Word, and MS Excel. That hold on the market was being challenged. Aside from the dot-com crash, the world of technology was booming with disruptions during his reign. Just to name a few, the exploding popularity of the internet, cloud computing, digitization of media, smartphones, and tablets.

On the outside, though the company's market share of operating systems fell from 96 percent when he took over to 35 percent when he exited, he actually tripled annual revenue from 23 billion to nearly 78 billion. On the inside, however, during his fourteen-year tenure, Ballmer went the other way with Microsoft instead of going back to its start-up roots. He created a culture of groupthink, failure avoidance, leadership aggression, and focus on individual experts vs. establishing the team as the base unit of success. Innovation was reactive and exploration was erratic through hit-and-miss acquisitions. As a result, Microsoft was not cool anymore.

In 2012, Kurt Massey, a former senior marketing manager shared his experience: "I see Microsoft as technology's answer to Sears. In the '40s, '50s, and '60s, Sears nailed it. It was top-notch, but now it's just a barren wasteland. And that's Microsoft. The company just isn't cool anymore" (Eichenwald 2012).

In comes Satya Nadella on the CEO scene. Though he grew within the management ranks of Microsoft, he turns the ship around by jumping on a new S-curve. Instead of letting product innovation be the driver for change, he goes deeper and focuses on changing the underlying culture. He encourages his peers and his organization to follow a growth mindset path. The old "know-it-all" paradigm is shed and replaced by a "learn-it-all" mindset.

Comparison of a know-it-all versus a learn-it-all management culture

KNOW-IT-ALL PARADIGM	LEARN-IT-ALL PARADIGM
Listen-to-fix or listen-to-win	Listen-to-improve
Leans in to prove I am right	Leans in with thoughtful reflection
Defensive and guarded	Intellectually humble and open
Me-focused	We-focused
Stays on familiar grounds	Explores the new

Adapted from A. Horstmeyer (2021, Intrinsic Curiosity, LLC)

Curiosity can support both incremental innovation from within as well as disruptive innovation from the fringes of the organization. Let's explore indeed the role of curiosity and the innovation appetite of companies in the next chapter. We will see curiosity is a force for good, yet fragile if not managed intentionally.

The Big Ideas

Successful companies and leaders are maintaining a healthy balance between exploration and exploitation in their strategy process.

The twenty-first century is the century of ideas. Given the challenges we have had in the last twenty years, it has become clear we need to ask new questions and derive new answers to face the challenges we are faced with.

Companies focusing on exploitation and disregarding exploration survive for as long as the environment does not change. The turmoil we have experienced in our societies during COVID-19 and the changes we have experienced in our industries in the last twenty years are clear indicators that companies need to start rethinking whether to hang on to old certainties.

When speaking to thought leaders and asking them what they think the corporate fabric will look like in the future, all of them predict change will accelerate even more. Elliott Masie, founder of the Masie Institute, summed it up nicely. He predicts "innovation will come from smaller companies, and they will come from anywhere on the planet."

Awareness of our twentieth century management frameworks helps us to look at the present with new eyes. The mental models that got us this far will not be the ones taking us into the future.

Curiosity is the required mindset for start-up entrepreneurs to kick-start an enterprise and for corporate leaders to help their organizations jump to the next generation of S-curves.

Questions for Reflection

- How well is curiosity embedded in your corporate strategy and how can this be improved?

- Do you focus your strategy on extending your known world or are you going beyond?

- Is strategy an activity that happens at headquarters or broadly across the organization?

- Where do you situate yourself on the exploration/exploitation scale?

- Are you ahead of the S-curve in your industry?

10

"WHAT IF?" INNOVATION AND CURIOSITY

———

"It is unbelievable how much you don't know about the game you've been playing all your life."

—MICKEY MANTLE, AMERICAN BASEBALL PLAYER

What about creating computer applications to help with diagnosing the headache of a patient?

CURIOSITY AND INNOVATION IN HEALTHCARE

Imagine you are a neurologist specializing in headaches. During the COVID-19 lockdown, you are unable to see your patients. Without consultations, you cannot diagnose or help them, and this will continue for as long as the lockdown lasts. Unlike other fields of medicine, the only tool neurologists have for pain diagnosis and treatment is the spoken word between the doctor and the patient.

According to Dr. Nicolas Vandenbussche, neurologist at the Ghent University Hospital in Belgium: "There are no tests, no monitoring equipment, no bloodwork or brain fluid tests available. Only language we have at our disposal with our patients." Neurologists often refer to the phrase "My language is my scalpel" to underscore this.

A headache is not a headache and diagnosing with only dialogue requires finesse and expertise. The doctor confirms, "There are two hundred different types of headaches people suffer from, each requiring a different diagnosis and a different treatment. For instance, migraine is very different from cluster headache." Migraines are the second biggest discomfort people suffer from after lower backaches. Around the world, one billion people suffer from it every year.

Given the complexity of the condition, the limitations of only language for diagnostics and the long waiting lists for seeing specialists, Dr. Vandenbussche shared, "Indeed, it takes on average two years before people are diagnosed correctly. This is a pity. The earlier the diagnosis, the faster recovery for patients." In comes COVID-19 and a lockdown. All consults with patients halt abruptly. What do you do?

You become curious. You dig deep. You explore what you know and what you don't know. You try to remember connections of the past, even irrelevant ones. In short, you try to come up with potential solutions to a new problem. How do you help patients in this new normal? It might be an opportunity to think outside the box and design a new approach. This was what Dr. Nicolas Vandenbussche thought.

"What if computers can help us with speed and accuracy in the early diagnosis?"

"What if instead of talking to patients, we invite them to write down what they feel and how they experience their discomfort?"

"What if that computer then analyzes the use of single words and combinations of words the patient writes down?"

"Would this help?"

A concept was born. In the spring of 2020, Dr. Vandenbussche worked with an IT company to create an algorithm to explore these ideas. This new idea is still in its early stages, yet results with patients have been promising in terms of reduction in diagnosis delay and an earlier improvement in the quality of life for the patient.

An unintended result has also been improvement in diagnosis accuracy. Computers can recognize patterns doctors might miss. Dr. Vandenbussche shared, "Patients often talk about their discomfort in roundabout ways and interchange the words like headache and pain. Doctors then try to derive meaning from the patient's description to decide on a diagnosis. A computer has no emotions and can pick up subtle use of words and word combinations not always apparent to humans. The algorithm identified clear distinctions between the use of headache and pain."

The use of the word "ache" is often related to internal sensations while "pain" is more often used in combination with an external cause. "Ache" is more often used when people migraine. Cluster headache patients, on the other hand, describe their condition more as "pain." Patients who suffer cluster headaches describe their type of pain as "hot pokes behind their eyes." A subtle difference the computer can help with when studying the texts of patients and a potentially extra aid for doctors to improve their care. (Additionally, in the Dutch language, "ache" is also used to describe the sensation of pain; so, the difference between the combined "head pain" and the single "pain" is even smaller.)

It all started from a challenge, an open-ended question, an idea, and a drive to solve it. The twenty-first century is the century of ideas. Given the challenges we have had in the last twenty years, it has become clear we need to ask new questions and derive new answers to face the challenges we are faced with. Curiosity and innovation go hand in hand, with curiosity being in the driver's seat. If you want to innovate, you need to encourage curiosity.

We have the choice to perpetuate the past, radically reinvent the future, or find a balance between the two. If you want innovation to meet new challenges, you need curiosity.

IS INNOVATION HARD?

In 2021, according to an innovation survey by the Boston Consulting Group, the innovation focus by CEOs showed "a 10-percentage-point increase, to 75 percent, in executives reporting innovation is a top-three priority at their companies. A third of them point to it as the number one priority" (Boston Consulting Group 2021).

The authors in the report also clarify, "Coming out of COVID-19, companies want—and need—to innovate. But too few are ready to rise to the challenge. Successful innovation takes three things—making innovation a priority, committing investment and talent to it, and being ready to transform investment into results."

That few companies truly embrace innovation was also confirmed to me by Kurt Verweire, strategy professor at the Vlerick Business School in Belgium. "Regardless of the rhetoric, CEOs are often less serious about innovation than they make others believe. Exploitation clearly trumps exploration."

According to Yury Boshyk, CEO and founder of Global Executive Learning and Business Driven Action Learning (BDAL), the appetite for curiosity and innovation depends on the following three dimensions:

1. **The type of organizational culture they embrace**. He distinguishes between four organizational cultures: hierarchical, family-based, market-facing, and ad hoc or opportunistic cultures. Curiosity and innovation have the most chance to be enabled in market-facing cultures and ad hoc environments. Market-facing cultures are curious because they rely on the outside-in sources of information and perspectives. This flows into the organization to guide their ongoing operations and innovation. Ad hoc cultures are often start-ups and have curiosity embedded in their build-adapt-learn cycles, which is inherently part of their organizational DNA. Hierarchical and family-based organizations, on the other hand, value conformity and obedience more.

One very large company based in Germany, but active in most countries, once described its company culture as demanding "anticipated obedience"—something the new CEO wanted to change.

2. **The types of questions leaders ask.** Many leaders prefer closed questions to open-ended ones. They prefer to ask: "Why didn't you do this?" or "Have you checked that?" rather than "'Help me understand the assumptions you made in this project." He shared, "McDonnell Douglas was struggling with innovation projects several years back until leadership started to intentionally ask open-ended questions. The deeper insights the answers created and the empowering effect of new questions on strategies increased innovation dramatically."

3. **The prevailing culture of the country.** "In the end, it depends on what kind of system or ecosystem you are embedded in. For example, the North American capitalist model endorses short-term thinking, share-holders reward senior management on the basis of short-term performance. Often the company is purely thought of as an economic unit-distinguishing between business *and* society." The European capitalist model, on the other hand, demands more social responsibility, supports more long-term thinking, and assigns pro-portionally larger value to employees—thus viewing business as being *in* society. According to Dr. Boshyk, companies have a choice to go against the prevailing current regardless of their country of origin. He shared the example of Johnson & Johnson. Since the start

of the company and the adoption of their "standards of leadership," it has been clear, patients, healthcare professionals, and employees come before shareholders in the value system adopted by the company. It is important to note, in its history of 134 years, it has been profitable almost every quarter. Moreover, it is the most admired company internationally as described in *Fortune Magazine*'s "2021 World's Most Admired Companies" list.

The perception of the employees in describing their employers as innovative is a noteworthy dimension. In my research findings, I have noticed when judging their environment as being innovative or not, a higher sensitivity is to be found by employees below the age of thirty. These younger employees are twice as critical about their company's desire for innovation when compared to their older peers. They are also less inclined to say their employer is ready to move in different directions from competition and appraise their organizations as less open than they would like them to be. Interestingly, the same demographic is twice as likely to say they are micromanaged compared to their older colleagues.

CULTURE INNOVATION AT SBER

Organizational innovation comes in different formats: business model innovation, culture innovation, product innovation, and process innovation. What they have in common is an underlying need to change the status quo and curiosity to ask different questions. The curious mindset leading to innovation starts at the top.

We have been speaking about the successes and pitfalls of organizational innovation and its link to curiosity in earlier chapters. You will remember the example when Satya Nadella, CEO of Microsoft, took over the helm from Steve Ballmer in February 2014. Mr. Nadella changed his organization from a know-it-all to a learn-it-all culture, a necessary step he believed to rekindle the company's lost desire to innovate.

Changing the culture was a means to an end. It was a strategy to give a much-needed boost to the way Microsoft created the necessary conditions to make the company great again. A reset was needed. Microsoft is not the only company that did this.

What would you do if you are head of a large bank faced with disruption in the economy, the rise of internet banking, cryptocurrency, and rapidly declining visitors to your branches? Would you address the challenge with fear or with curiosity? The leaders at Sber chose the path of curiosity.

Sberbank is Russia's oldest and largest bank. It is particularly dominant in the field of individual savings accounts, holding about 65 percent of household deposits nationwide. The company holds assets of around four hundred billion dollars and sits at a market value of about sixty-seven billion dollars. It serves more than one hundred million active banking clients. It claims 18,000 branches, primarily in Russia.

The changes in the economic system in Russia, the rise of internet banking and opportunities beyond banking have pushed the bank to create the largest transformation in its 179-year history. In September 2020, Sberbank, Russia's state-owned but stock-listed bank, rebranded to "Sber" as it invests big in its revamp to shine as a technology company. "It's a huge investment, not a big investment," the bank's chief technology officer, David Rafalovsky told Reuters. "We've always had a chip on our shoulder. We believe we are a technology company with a banking license" (Marrow 2020). In fact, they are going beyond their banking roots and have been investing heavily in a multitude of industries such as marketplaces, e-health, logistics, pharma, and more, and hosting more than six labs doing fundamental research on robotics, neurology, etc.

The changes at Sber highlight the dialectic relationship between the past and the present, the company and the society, the individual and the environment, improving the known world and exploring the new unknown. Traditionally, the pre-perestroika communist elite was more in favor of conformity rather than divergent thinkers.

In the West, we called these divergent thinkers dissidents. Even though on the political front, unity, obedience, and compliance to a single party is still the norm, the economic upheaval since the 1990s in the Soviet Union seems to have created the right conditions for new ideas to emerge. Some of these new ideas come straight from the West, yet according to Oliver Kempkens, chief product officer for Sber's banking division, increasingly such ideas are home-grown and are radically different from what is taught in Western MBA schools.

The key goal of the company's 2023 strategy is to achieve a whole new level of competitiveness to compete against global technology companies, while maintaining their status as the best bank for individuals and companies. Interestingly, the first rule of the Sber guiding principles is: it is more than just a bank. While other banks in the West are quickly becoming technology companies, Sber seems to have passed this stage already and is conquering new territories beyond banking.

An important guiding principle underlying their strategy is their systemic ecosystem thinking. Herman Gref, CEO, chairman of the executive board, SberBank shares on the company's website: "We don't see our businesses as separate assets, but rather think of them as parts of an integrated business model, the ecosystem" (Sberbank 2020).

Oliver Kempkens highlighted for me how the speed of change was much faster in Russia than he had experienced in Western countries. According to him, there is more openness in trying out new things in Russian enterprises vis-à-vis companies in the United States. In Russia, there is less maturity in the overall system, hence less rigidity, thus allowing for more innovation and greenfield thinking.

Sber has been pioneering blockchain and adopting digital payment gateways before many of its international peers started. It is also interesting to note once Sber's leadership decided to focus on technology, they have been fast in diversifying their investments beyond banking, but also diversifying the mandatory trainings in the bank. Every employee needs to take classes to understand the foundations of Python.

According to Mr. Kempkens, Sber's drive for increased innovation comes at a price. It is creating friction with the traditional risk averse and cautious leadership culture of the banking core of their business. But Sber's leadership is set on this new strategic agenda.

Employees see that leadership appreciates curiosity, and there is an increasing tendency for middle management to actively embrace innovation.

—Oliver Kempkens

ACCELERATING THE RURAL ECONOMY IN AFRICA

Not every company needs to innovate on a global scale and prepare for a multitude of different contexts. Sber is primarily focusing on its Russian home market. Before a company can create scalability on a regional or global level, it needs to be differentiating in its home market.

Most small and medium-sized companies are operating locally. For them, curiosity means being open to novel ideas and doing things differently than the competition. It also means to read market signals before anyone else does, and then implement faster and better than the competitors. Very curious organizations go beyond and look for opportunities where others don't. As we will see, Baobab Express actively tries to collaborate with multiple stakeholders (even with competition) and is designing novel services for their customers.

Baobab Express is a bus company revolutionizing the transportation business and accelerating the rural economy in Benin. The company started as a project of a number of Belgian investors who wanted to invest in a sustainable and profitable long-term social project.

Under the charismatic guidance of Kris Van Assche, they helped create a differentiating and profitable bus company in Benin—not that they had a blueprint to rely on.

> When we started, we had no knowledge of the market, we knew directionally what we wanted to achieve, yet had no preconceived ideas about how to do it. We knew we did not want to compete on price, but on quality of service and safety. We knew we needed to be open-minded and flexible, empower the local colleagues, and see the other players in the market as collaboration partners rather than competitors.
>
> —Kris Van Assche

The initial differentiating measure for the company was to focus on punctuality of departures and arrivals. Culturally, punctuality was not high on the agenda of the many minibus companies who would wait until their buses were full before they started. Once customers understood Baobab Express meant reliability in terms of timeliness, business picked up nicely. They started in 2013 with six minibuses; in 2021, they own twenty-four full-fledged Volvo buses.

Building on this success, the company has been looking at ways to act as an accelerator for the community. Their principle is to empower local management where Kris Van Assche sees himself as a mentor. They have been actively working with competition to collaborate, for instance having smaller competitors specialize in last mile transportation.

With the money they earned in their bus venture, they worked with a local team to create an app to allow for prepaid ticketing. They are even investigating the feasibility of using the batteries of electric scooters to be charged in the bus terminals and to serve as batteries for home use for off-grid villages. This has especially enabled women entrepreneurs to be able to drive their electric scooters to the bus terminal for sales of produce in the city. At the same time, they can use their scooter batteries for lighting their houses in the evening.

They are proving curiosity leads to meaningful and profitable growth and development of all stakeholders.

FUTURE LABS AT GRUNDFOS

Workplace curiosity is not the birthright of start-ups. Many established organizations embracing innovation prove this. The industrial Danish water pump company Grundfos is one of them. Grundfos is one of the global leaders in the professional and home segments.

I had the pleasure to get to know two innovation leaders at Grundfos through a curiosity project I did for the company: Lars Spicker Olesen, group director, Circular Water at the Grundfos Future Lab, and Fredrik Östbye, group vice president and head of Future Lab.

They shared with me, Grundfos prides itself on having a culture that balances thinking and doing, curiosity and agility, innovation and operationalization. An industrial technical company at heart, the company has been adopting the following gates for managing innovation structurally:

IDEATION
↓
CONCEPTUALIZATION
↓
INCUBATION
↓
VIABLE BUSINESS
↓
SCALING

They are implementing this approach not only for incremental innovation in their core product lines, but also engage in radical innovation in new domains. All innovations they do are plotted in one of the nine squares of the nine-block innovation they have adopted.

Nine block model for innovation

Like most companies, Grundfos is going through stages. At times, the focus is more on exploitation; at other times, there is an effort to balance innovation and exploitation. The company is deeply aware leadership agendas and strategic considerations can get consumed by the present, firefighting, portfolio discussions, internal meetings, etc.

For Grundfos, it is the task of the board to ensure the CEO and senior management are keeping innovation high on the strategic agenda. About ten years ago, their board indeed warned the senior team, the company had not been an industrial trendsetter like it used to be. They urged the senior management team to trigger their organization into exploration beyond engaging primarily in continuous improvement in their core businesses.

This led to not only a renewed focus on embracing innovation as an integral part of their strategy across their business lines, but it also led to adopting an expansive view of innovation. It created the impetus to create the Grundfos "Future Lab": an internal engine for innovation and disruption beyond the incremental innovation the various business lines are engaged in.

The Future Lab is highlighting the importance Grundfos pays to having a centralized disruption unit, a safe playground to explore new horizons, "where no one has gone before." While the various business lines engage in incremental innovation, the Future Lab focuses on radical innovation in core, adjacent, and transformational innovation of their nine-block model.

It is important to note the scope of the Future Lab is not only to think of new products or solutions but take an end-to-end process view of ideation >incubation >viable business >sales. In Fredrik Östbye's words, "With Future Lab, we are mimicking a start-up: there is no leaner way to innovate than the start-up way."

This is an important point Lars Olesen underscores. Exploration and exploitation are different sides of the same coin, each with its own characteristics.

Start-up companies tend to be better at exploration; large companies better at exploitation. Those start-ups who are unable to operationalize and scale their big idea perish. Likewise, traditional companies typically are better at operational excellence and efficiency. For as long as the market remains stable, they thrive. Once, however, the market becomes more volatile, they become vulnerable.

HOW TO CREATE A CURIOUS INNOVATION CULTURE

When analyzing the best practices in creating curious innovation cultures, we can distill the following dimensions:

- **Embrace a strategy to exploit and explore**. Both dimensions are important, and both need dedication and strategic focus. The Grundfos business lines focus on exploitation and both incremental and evolutionary innovation. This is complemented by the Future Lab, which takes care of exploring radical innovation in core product lines, adjacent solutions, and transformational new areas. Grundfos' innovation strategy differentiates between short-, middle-, and long-term innovation horizons along the nine-block model as described above.

- **Focus and follow through**. Avoid costly, erratic, and demotivating start/stop/change of projects. Create incentives to link sales and innovation teams. For example, ensure salespeople are keen to sell new products and solutions.

- **Focus on culture**. Create a culture of openness and failure acceptance. Drive innovation behavior all the way from the top. Ensure curious behavior is also captured in the business key performance indicators. A curious culture embraces openness, the desire to welcome change, and courage to go in different directions vs. competition. Realizing obedience to reporting lines can be more important than adding value, Grundfos has created communities of talent. Specialists are connected in expertise pools and assigned to business projects. These groups are managed by people managers responsible for the wellness of the community, not for the delivery of the various projects.

- **Embrace diversity**. Not all people are good at everything. Let the explorers explore, the exploiters exploit, celebrate both, yet create linkages between the explorers and exploiters. Grundfos realized their recognition processes were linked only to promotion, and promotion meant becoming a manager, even if it was not the strength of the person or her/his passion. They realized this did not support the exploration mindset they endorsed and looked for alternative ways to recognize people, such as, creating technical career tracks next to management tracks.

- **Create productive tension in the system**. Avoid groupthink and confirmation bias; allow people to challenge each other's projects and thinking and create an intentional culture where senior management is challenged by the board and their employees.

- **Play with the time you got.** This is especially true for business-to-business ("b2b") industrial product application companies. Consistency and persistence over time is more important than speed-to-market.

In the next chapter, we will see curiosity is not only relevant for strategy creation and innovation. It has distinct influence on the human side of businesses. Let's turn now to how curiosity leads to employee engagement and productivity, and how and why curiosity is important in the human resources space.

The Big Ideas

Organizational innovation comes in different formats: business model innovation, culture innovation, product innovation, and process innovation. What they have in common is an underlying need to change the status quo and curiosity to ask different questions.

When reflecting on curiosity, it helps to analyze the types of questions leaders ask and the surrounding organizational culture as well as the prevailing economic mindset.

The curiosity mindset leading to innovation starts at the top. The positive role modelling of senior management ensures middle management also embraces curiosity and innovation. My research has found, for large scale organizations, it is not uncommon for middle management to be four times less ready to say curiosity and innovation is an important part of what they do.

In the same organization, the generation of professionals under thirty years of age are two times as uncertain about their company's desire for innovation and are two times less ready to say their employer is ready to move in different directions from the competition when compared to their older peers.

Companies not only need to have an innovation agenda, but also an innovation culture where individuals and teams are given the time and space to explore small and big improvements.

Curiosity and innovation go hand in hand, with curiosity being in the driver's seat. If you want to innovate, you need to intentionally encourage curiosity. If the curiosity is narrow, this will lead to incremental innovation of the existing products or services. Broad curiosity leads to more radical innovation.

Questions for Reflection

- Where do you rate your company's innovation on the nine-block model listed above?

- When looking at your own department, how easy is it to introduce and adopt new ideas?

- How would you describe the innovation culture in your organization?

- Is your company willing to move in different directions from your competition?

- What would you advise to your CEO when asked what the company should start/stop/continue in the space of curiosity-driven innovation?

11

HR'S ROLE IN EMBRACING CURIOSITY

———

*"Hire people who are better than you are, then leave
them to get on with it. Look for people who will aim for
the remarkable, who will not settle for the routine. "*
—DAVID OGILVY, FOUNDER OF OGILVY & MATHER

Who do we typically promote in our organizations? We did a
thought experiment in Chapter 9. Who would you promote,
Jeff or Mary? Jeff is the candidate who is good at doing what
he is asked, the conformist. Mary represents the archetype
of the candidate who performs equally well yet explores new
terrains, the curious professional.

I often do this simple thought experiment with leaders in
workshops. The answer I get from them is often: in our company, we would promote Jeff, even though we know we should
promote Mary.

It highlights our underlying mindsets for at least a couple of reasons.

1. It brings out the difference between how we perceive theory and practice. At a conceptual level, we might think of our organization as a curious place to work. I am not denying this. What the experiment shows is there is a difference between theory and practice. Though we can all find examples of why our organization is indeed encouraging curiosity, we can also find examples of processes and practices where curiosity is not supported.

2. The thought experiment also highlights a deeper psychological need for stability. We—and the processes we create once we are in a state of routine—prefer stability, predictability, and risk avoidance over its opposite. In such a scenario, efficiency trumps curiosity.

3. When profit is the sole driver in the company, HR's practices are there to maximize profits too. Everything supports this premise and everything else is deprioritized. Once companies move from a single "P" (profit) focus to a triple "P" (profit, people, planet), things often change.

Beyond promotions, how well are our companies' HR practices endorsing, supporting, or even actively pursuing curiosity throughout the employee life cycle? How well is curiosity a factor in recruiting, onboarding, promotion, rewards, learning and development, and offboarding?

THE CASE FOR JOB ROTATION

In my own work with companies, I have found individual curiosity levels decrease when people have been in the same role for three years or longer. What aggravates this is, at that juncture in time, these employees have become more critical of the curious nature of their company. They indicate it is harder to experiment, stick out one's neck, and engage in improvement pilots; they even appreciate their direct manager less than people in their first three years of tenure.

A strange addendum to this finding is once people are five years or longer in the same role, they again become more positive about their environment. This is, however, a false positive. The results show employees are overly careful to protect their job security and play it safe and go with the flow rather than rock the system with some new idea or suggestion and risk being noticed.

Professor van Dam could easily relate to this finding for many organizations, yet not for McKinsey. According to him, employees at McKinsey are expected to move into a new role every two to three years. Given the global reach, multiple roles, and the multitude of industrial segments the company serves, this is a policy the proactively enacts upon, even for the CEO.

WE KNOW YOU HAVE A CHOICE

Let's focus on recruitment. The recruitment process is one good way to gauge the openness and thus curiosity level of an organization. We all have experienced this process at one time in our lives. When reflecting on this experience, think whether the company that recruited you was more interested in your skills, your curious mind, or both.

When speaking to a group of Brazilian professionals, one of the participants shared with me a recruitment experience. She had mentioned to the recruiter that she saw herself as a curious professional to which the recruiter had reacted negatively. At that moment, she knew she did not want to work for them anymore.

The Brazilian recruiter in the above example was probably not aware of the research showing that curiosity and effort combined have just as much effect on performance than intelligence. Measuring the curiosity level of a new applicant may be a better predictor of her ability to perform well in a job. Once hired, curiosity helps the professional learn faster in the new environment and engage faster with new colleagues. Because of her higher inclination for openness, she will also be more open to change and be at ease in dealing with unfamiliar work (Gruber 2019).

Personally, I have always looked for people with an edge to join my team. In recruiting people, a standard question I ask is: "What is your passion outside of work?" If people have nothing to say or mumble something generic like traveling or watching movies, I become less interested. When their eyes light up and they start talking about being part of a local community work or a passionate hobby they engage in, then they have more of my attention. I believe strongly that people who are intentionally curious at home will also be curious at work. These people will not only bring new perspectives to the table, but they also have superior ways to recharge their batteries for work through their passion.

What I have found in my research is curious companies are also more intentional about their HR processes and practices. In the specific case of recruitment, they spend time planning for the best possible candidate experience, are intentional in standing out from others to recruit the best, are rigorous, yet transparent in their selection criteria, treat potential employees with respect, and project an authentic picture of the company and its values from beginning to end. They are also data driven.

We already discussed the Google Highway 101 billboard example in the introduction as a best practice. Let's look at some other examples.

QUICK RELEASE

"We know many candidates in our industry have a choice; we also know the best candidates have lots of employment choices," shared Alex Evans, recruiting manager for Quick Release, a two-hundred-person-strong processes and technology niche consultancy for the automotive industry. Being a medium-sized company and not a global brand, they realize they need to try harder to find good people. To ensure they could attract the best candidates to their organization, they created an innovative recruitment approach with the candidate experience front and center. This includes process transparency and the ability for both the candidate and the company to manage the process as equals. The target group for candidates is typically recent graduates: the GenZ demographic.

This is how they engage with people. After the initial application form, the candidate is invited to self-record a video answering several screening questions as proposed by the company. The candidate can prepare the video in her own time and re-record if so desired. After submission, the company proposes a forty-eight-hour turnaround at which a decision is made to invite the candidate to an assessment center. The assessment center is not only meant to test candidates further, it is also an opportunity for candidates to get a feel for the culture of openness within the company and ask questions, and ultimately an opportunity for the company to build confidence as an excellent place to work. Openness to Quick Release is also about sharing where things went wrong. The successful candidates are then invited to a value-based interview with one of the business leaders.

This process of mutual equality and honest communication has allowed Quick Release to hire top-notch candidates. Alex Evans' definition of great candidates is not candidates who had great results in school; rather, it is candidates who bring energy, passion, a growth mindset, and curiosity to the team. Not surprisingly, their employee brand promise is "curiosity, energy, and passion."

BRING YOUR CURIOSITY TO LIFE AT MERCK KGAA, DARMSTADT, GERMANY

Merck KGaA, Darmstadt, Germany has been adopting intentional curiosity since 2015. According to Christine Blum-Heuser, associate director of the company's Brand Initiative, the company has adopted the concept of curiosity as the gel between their strategy and corporate values: "Curious minds dedicated to human progress." With this phrase, they encourage all fifty-eight thousand employees in over sixty-six countries to question the status quo and to think beyond the limits of one's own individual area.

In talent acquisition, the company's employer value proposition "bring your curiosity to life" is connected to their overall brand promise. Henriette Fink, an employer branding specialist at the company's headquarters in Darmstadt, mentioned to me that their earlier brand promise was "make great things happen." Ms. Fink and her colleagues found in their ongoing research that the old brand promise was not differentiating enough. According to Ms. Fink: "Everybody in the industry is using the same words such as innovation, collaboration, or change."

According to her, the biggest impact since the change of their employer branding in 2017 was raising the awareness of Merck KGaA, Darmstadt, Germany as a good company to work with. More importantly, the focus on curiosity has resulted in the company being viewed as positively different from its industry peers. Both the quantity and quality of applicants has improved significantly at above-industry standards.

Interestingly, Ms. Fink mentioned they have found curiosity is not linked to the younger demographics like millennials or Gen Z, but to all age groups. This in comparison to concepts like sustainability and purpose, which resonates more with the younger generation of employees.

The company has not only changed its key messaging on their corporate website, but recruiters have also been trained extensively on talking about curiosity and have online tools at their disposal to keep current. They are encouraged to gauge the curiosity level of candidates.

TIME TO EXPLORE

It is fair to say Google is a curious (and innovative) company, at least when we consider their intellectual curiosity. The company has been exploring new horizons: from eyeglasses to self-driving cars and much more. They also have been exploring the right environment for people to thrive; they provide free food, have in-house laundry cleaning, and have created relaxation rooms. In short: they want to create a superlative environment for their employees, so they don't have to worry about a number of things like food and laundry, but instead focus on creating magic for the company.

This does not mean they are perfect. In my interview with Teddy Frank, a renowned corporate culture specialist, she mentioned Google was indeed excelling on curiosity leading to product innovation, yet, in her view, they were not excelling equally high on their empathic dimension of curiosity. "At a fundamental level, Google has not yet solved the issue of burnout among its employees."

Could it be all the amenities Google introduced are part of the problem, and it encourages employees to focus even more on work instead of on finding a work-life balance?

They might not be perfect, yet Google's founders, Sergey Brin and Larry Page, have instilled a simple process to make sure they not only get the most out of their employees on company-initiated projects, they also allow employees to initiate and work on pet projects employees themselves feel passionate about. This process even has a name: "The 20 Percent Project" (Schrage 2013).

The concept is not new and was started by 3M as early as 1948. 3M's management allowed their staff to dedicate up to 15 percent of their paid hours to pursue a personal interest. Googlers—the common name for employees of Google—are allocated 20 percent of their paid work time to pursue personal projects. The objective of the program is clear: it is to create an empowering environment where every employee can explore new areas of intrinsic interest. As a result, the company can tap into the vast intellectual and creative potential of Googlers and ultimately increase company potential. Susan Wojcicki created AdSense in her free time and Krishna Bharat created Google News as an individual pursuit and hobby for Google (Murphy 2020).

It has been commonly assumed Google's free e-mail service "Gmail" was also created in the 20 percent tinkering time by Googler Paul Buchheit. This is not accurate. Gmail was officially put on the roadmap by Google's management and was not the surprising result of an inquisitive single individual (McCracken 2014). In any case, Google thrives on smart, inquisitive, creative, and curious engineers who can make a difference.

Not all companies are as forthcoming in giving autonomy to their employees as Google and 3M. Indeed, when running workshops with teams, feedback I often get is bottom-up new ideas are not always appreciated by the bosses above. I often hear some hidden sarcasm from people when they share management's feedback to their suggestions, such as:

- Time is money.

- I am not paying you to think.

- Coming up with improvement suggestions is above your paygrade.

- Nice idea. Why don't you explore this in your free time?

What these comments have in common is a preference for keeping the status quo and a reluctance for exploration. Not all companies are stifling the creative juices of their employees with restrictive HR policies. On the contrary, I have observed several companies take positive new directions to encourage employees to explore beyond their daily roles and have been adopted by more companies. I'd like to mention specifically one company that caught my attention: PepsiCo.

PepsiCo's chief learning officer, Molly Nagler, mentioned to me her company has created an internal project marketplace where employees can apply for joining temporary and part-time stretched assignment projects outside of their own department and comfort zone. So, a person working in manufacturing can apply to work on a marketing project and spend four hours per week learning something new, engaging with new colleagues and bringing new perspectives to the project.

I have been mentoring one of the PepsiCo colleagues from their change management practice who had applied to such a part time temporary project for PepU, short for PepsiCo University. The project was about how to structure a curiosity curriculum across the different levels in the organization.

IN SEARCH OF A NEW EQUILIBRIUM

Perry Timms is a founder of a company helping companies to redesign their HR practices. I met him at a conference in Berlin where we were both speaking. He had just started his own consulting company helping HR teams embrace a new paradigm of people management. He was speaking about innovation in human resources. I was speaking on innovation in the space of learning and development. One of the underlying beliefs he shared was organizations can become better workplaces if only they change their paradigm toward a more humanistic one.

"Parent/Child" and "Adult/Adult" are terms used in a branch of psychology called transactional analysis. I came across this powerful concept many years ago when reading Dr. Eric Berne's 1972 book, *What Do You Say After You Say Hello?* He describes how our unconscious scripts not only direct our own personality, but also manage how we engage with others. These scripts are the mental models or filters through which we view the world. When observing the employer–employee relationship, we can distill a parent/child dynamic in traditional companies.

In such a dynamic, the company behaves as the overbearing yet caring parent who decides what is good for the employee, gives feedback yet does not ask for feedback in return, and creates a climate of dependence and demands loyalty. The other side of this equation—that employee behaves as a "child"—is reflected in the following behavior. In this case, the employee is fine to let the higher-ups make decisions and prefers to focus on following orders rather than making decisions, linking her/his social worth to a high degree to her/his position in the organization.

The alternative Perry proposes is one where both the company and the employee behave as equals, as adults. The company behaves not as a paternalistic parent, but as a balanced adult engaged in a dialogue of equals with the employee who also behaves as an adult. In recent years, we have observed this trend in an increase of young professionals choosing to set up their own companies and offer their services to companies rather than engage in an—more restrictive—employee relationships with their companies.

To foster a curious culture, the role of the human resources department is crucial in the way they design, measure, and evaluate proactive workplace policies and practices helping to attract and retain talent with skills and competencies necessary for growth and sustainability. Some examples of the changing HR landscape Perry described across the employee lifecycle journey are listed in the below graph.

Traditional Versus New Approaches to HR

	FROM	TO
PRE-ONBOARDING	Marketing investments are reserved for product marketing. Low investment on new employee branding and minimal communication about what the company has to offer to future employees.	Creating a positive image early at the first and in every interaction and a brand of curiosity of difference and adventure. A clear focus on clarifying the deeper purpose and societal role of the organization.
RECRUITMENT	An employee needs to sell herself to a hard-to-get company. Monologue rather than dialogue. Employee at mercy of the company processes.	A dance of equals exploring a match/inclusive approach.
ONBOARDING	Trying to conform people as quickly as possible to the company norm, one size fits all.	Respect for the previous experience of the employee. Personalization of the onboarding process.
TEAMS	Long term intact teams. Expectation to fit in and follow.	Fluid and agile ever-changing project teams. No continuous fixed teams. Expectation of good collaboration ethic, curious about work and others.
CAREER MANAGEMENT	Only way "up" is by becoming a manager.	Squiggly career: career can go in any direction, it does not have to only go up. Less status-led. This new approach will attract people who have a lesser need to be identified with a fancy title but are able to stand on their own.
PERFORMANCE MANAGEMENT	Paternalistic approach: narrow objectives set by the organisation and the manager, no or little input by the employee.	Mutual exchange of adults.
LEARNING AND DEVELOPMENT	Just enough training provided to maintain the current job. Focus on courses.	Holistic development: training for the current and next job, employees are given time to explore interests and develop themselves.
PROMOTION	Up or out; promotion means recognition of the added value within a conformist paradigm.	Recognition that some roles are more strategic, more decision power, more financial risk—so some people might be more "senior" than others. Recognize everybody's path can be different.

REWARDS AND RECOGNITION	Monetary focus is only way to recognize people (i.e., focus on stocks and bonus and salary)—pay for performance.	Mix of monetary and non-monetary drivers, decided in dialogue by the employee within the framework provided by the employer. Instead of single monetary focus), alternatives are explored like time off, learning sabbatical, choose your own benefits (cafeteria model), performance plus curiosity (explore something new...)
EXIT	Referring to voluntary exit as an act of disloyalty and a forced exit as a shameful blemish on the shield of the employee.	Treat ex-employees like alumni who want to keep in contact with the old colleagues as well as the company, acceptance of fluidity of entry and exit.
SYSTEMS OF WORK	Build on process optimization and the most replicable practices that create a tightly woven set of acceptable practices.	Emergent, adaptive, and adjustable practices where appropriate that allow people to exert adaptive value and reflect changing parameters of external drivers and individual needs and that complement processes and systems that rightly remain replicable and hard-wired.

How do we develop employees and leaders to become more curious at work? We will cover in the next chapter how the learning and development function is supporting curiosity. We will also discuss what prevents learning and development teams from adopting curiosity in their growth and development plans. We will share best practices and suggest new strategies to redefine learning and development through the lens of curiosity.

The Big Ideas

Human resources teams in early adopter organizations are starting to shed their twentieth-century industrial skins and are creating more humanistic cultures where people can thrive to their full potential. These early adopter organizations are showing the way and prepare the path for others to follow.

For them, curiosity is not a simple slogan designed by marketing, but an expression of their intent. Merck KGaA, Darmstadt, Germany, for instance, since adopting curiosity as a key theme since 2015, have engaged in fundamental research on workplace curiosity with leading researchers and were looking for questions like: Can we measure curiosity? Can we influence it? In comparing their data between 2018 and 2020, they calculated the overall curiosity level of their employees is 13 percent higher than their competitors.

Curious organizations take advantage of adjusting things on two fronts. On the one hand, they ensure all people processes and practices reflect the deeper positive humanistic principles they cherish. They are refining their recruitment, onboarding, talent management, and even exit processes. On the other hand, they embrace a growth mindset attitude toward their employees and believe with the right training and active support, individuals can strengthen their curiosity mindset and learn tools to embrace curiosity as a power for good.

Curious human resources teams are passionate about data. They research data and act where needed. When they see individual productivity stagnates after three years and correlate this with a decline in individual curiosity of the employee, they recommend job rotation. They do this with all HR processes.

Questions for Reflection

- In your company, who would you promote in the end: Jeff or Mary?

- What would you say are the specific human resources processes supporting curiosity at work?

- Which human resources processes and practices inhibit curiosity?

- What small step would you advise your human resources team to shift the needle toward (even) more curiosity?

- What would you advise to your CEO as the single most important step to take to embrace curiosity (even) more?

12

DEVELOPING CURIOUS PEOPLE

———

"It takes curiosity to learn. It takes courage to unlearn. Learning requires the humility to admit what you don't know today. Unlearning requires the integrity to admit that you were wrong yesterday. Learning is how you evolve. Unlearning is how you keep up as the world evolves."

—ADAM GRANT, ORGANIZATIONAL
PSYCHOLOGIST, WHARTON SCHOOL

"What would it take to teach a group of young pupils in a deprived neighborhood and a substandard school?" was the question Erin Gruwell asked herself. Played by the actress Hilary Swank in the movie *Freedom Writers*, Erin Gruwell is a young teacher ready to do good and is unburdened by limiting beliefs. Instead of joining the ranks of her sarcastic teacher colleagues at her school, she embraced her students with all her positive might. In the process, she creates psychologically safe conditions conducive for learning to become possible even for the "lesser" students.

s have been blessed to be guided by an exemplary
er like Erin Gruwell. Many of us have had a good expe-
nce with a couple of passionate teachers throughout our
schooling days. We remember these teachers fondly. Most
of the time, we have erased the other teachers we enjoyed
early in life from our minds. The fact we make movies about
remarkable teachers is a sign they are more the exception
rather than the rule.

For Erin Gruwell, being a teacher was not a job; it was a
calling to make the lives of the young people entrusted to her
better and to enable her students to become better versions of
themselves. Her curiosity sparked the curiosity of her students.

We have spoken elsewhere about the positive effect of curiosity
on engagement, innovation, change acceptance, and productivity. The link of curiosity to learning is equally important:
curiosity primes our learning pump. When we are in a state
of curiosity, our minds prepare our brains to welcome new
information better and deeper. As a result, curious people
learn faster and remember better what they have learned.
When we are curious about a specific topic, we can learn and
remember unrelated topics better.

When we are not curious, or when we are forced to be curious, we will respond with resentment, boredom, or both, and
as a result, not learn. The more a company forces learning
on its employees, the more they create compliant and conformist doers. On the other hand, the more they empower
employees to learn what they need and want intrinsically, the
more they create curious, engaged, and productive thinkers
and doers.

It is good to be curious. It is also good to make people curious. Even better is when we train people on how to strengthen their curiosity muscle.

The research firm Gartner predicts only 20 percent of employees have the skills needed for both their current role and their future career (Gartner 2018).

We know the "half-life of skills" has been decreasing. A curious person in the fifteenth century like Leonardo da Vinci viewed knowledge as something permanent. Not anymore. Overall, the skills we learn in school only help us for the first five to ten years of our career. If we don't upskill ourselves, we become a cognitive dinosaur. In industries such as IT, old skills become redundant even faster.

WHAT IS HOLDING LEARNING AND DEVELOPMENT BACK?

When discussing the state of the L&D profession with Professor Nick van Dam of IE University, he made the analogy of the L&D function with the IT department. He shared, "Thirty years ago, the IT department was the tactical help desk you visited when your computer was broken, now they are one of the most strategic groups of the organization. L&D is still behaving as if they are the tactical help desk while they have the opportunity to transform themselves."

Elliott Masie, global authority on corporate learning answered this question eloquently. When we spoke, he identified four areas holding back learning and development teams in organizations.

- They confuse teaching with learning. L&D is structured as a scalable teaching environment benefiting the organization, not a scalable learning environment benefiting both the organization and the employees.

- Data-savviness and smartness. According to Mr. Masie, "Curiosity involves evidence and data. Why do you teach this course as a five-day course instead of a five-hour course? The answer in most cases will be because we have always done it this way. A data-smart answer would be: we tried it for five hours and we tried it for five days and here is what the evidence shows."

- Technology systems optimize delivery, not the experience of an individual. Technology is not consumer grade. "I have been beating up the Learning Management System (LMS) community for thirty years. They track whether you have followed a course, they don't tell whether you should watch the thirty-second, three-minute, or thirty-minute videos, read the pdf, or do something else—our systems don't enhance curiosity."

- Business sense. "Most of the L&D people are business naïve. I have not seen a single CLO become a Fortune 500 CEO. We *(L&D)* don't always get what the business is all about."

According to another equally respected thought leader, Donald H. Taylor, chair of the UK based Learning Technologies Conference, what is holding L&D back is the fact it is not innovative and future-oriented enough.

L&D is still too fond of its historic identity of creating and delivering courses. In the light of the changing landscape of content being freely available anywhere, the increased speed of doing business, tenure of employees is going down, the complex nature of reskilling, and the changing social contract and expectations between employees and employers all contribute, the traditional focus of L&D is ready for a change.

—Donald H. Taylor

Lori Niles-Hofmann, global learning strategist, echoes the above messages when sharing, "The most successful L&D teams are those who focus on culture instead of training, those who encourage a curiosity pull from the employees rather than a top-down compliance push for training."

Clearly, forward-thinking L&D groups in forward-thinking companies are proving Nick van Dam, Elliott Masie, Donald H. Taylor, and Lori Niles-Hofmann wrong, truth be told. The innovators, however, are more the exception than the rule, yet being early adopters, they show the rest how to shape innovative learning organizations. Many of the L&D groups are still laggards; they are more tactical than strategic, more pleasers than challengers, more reactive than proactive, and more course administrators than culture changers.

TEYA: BRAZILIAN INNOVATION

A good example of a forward-thinking L&D provider for me is the Brazilian company Teya. I have come to know their founder,

Alexandre Santille, well as a successful learning innovator and advisor. He shared with me one of his customer projects he was doing for a large agro-business customer. He was asked to do a train-the-trainer program to equip the technical trainers of his client company. When he and his team realized the assigned participants of this training program were appointed by their managers to become trainers rather than wanting to do it themselves, he set out on another trajectory.

He mapped the influencers in the organization and posited a simple question to everyone. "Who do you go to when you have a question?" What they did was to map the hidden potential of employees who were already sharing knowledge and were intrinsically pleased to do that. This led to a very different list of names of people than the experts who were nominated to become trainers. This initiative unveiled an important aspect of the learning culture of the company that was not hitherto visible to the L&D professionals.

When sharing these findings to the management of his client, they immediately saw the potential of their influencer population and agreed to change their approach. Mr. Santille shared an extra insight of this project: the "informal learning booster colleagues" were not necessarily the best experts in their areas. They were, however, the most willing to help and support their colleagues.

EVERY EMPLOYEE CONTRIBUTING TO COLLECTIVE KNOWLEDGE

The image L&D enjoys in many organizations is low, yet the challenge facing organizations in the space of creating a culture of employee-driven learning to support skilling, up-skilling, and especially reskilling are, however, daunting. The World Economic Forum has predicted 40 percent of the core skills of our current workers are expected to change in the next five years and 50 percent of all employees will need reskilling by 2025. Reskilling means radical change for both the individual as well as the organization. It involves, for instance, training a low-level call center employee into a machine learning expert.

It also means, L&D is the driver for learning culture change and challenges the status quo toward embracing curiosity at the organizational level as well as encouraging curiosity at the individual level.

A company carrying a high reputation when it comes to innovation in learning is Google. They have clearly gone beyond the paradigm that learning is all about creating and delivering courses to be consumed by employees. They turned this paradigm on its head and instead of treating corporate learning as consumption, they have made it also a function of contribution.

The idea is quite basic yet very powerful. It is built on the belief every employee has unique skills and experiences that can be beneficial for their peers. So instead of relying on external experts to teach programs, first the company checks whether they have internal resources who have the knowledge and are interested in sharing them. With their Googler2Googler program, they have created a culture of appreciating the knowledge and expertise of every employee and created a platform for employees to share their knowledge, even in non-business-related areas like mindfulness.

I have been replicating this philosophy in several companies with great success. In my own experience, the attendance at sessions delivered by peers is ten times greater as compared to the external speakers or trainers. Engagement to learn from a knowledgeable peer is also higher than learning from an external resource who may or may not be knowledgeable about the specific corporate context on the ground.

OPPORTUNITIES

Once we understand the power of empowered curiosity and learning, one could ask the question of why many organizations are giving lip-service to supporting growth and development for their employees and why they are not more demanding of their L&D teams, especially when the same CEOs say, they have a real skill challenge on their hands?

I have been a chief learning officer for Fortune 200 companies for the biggest part of my career and have observed huge differences in how companies frame, value, and encourage learning and growth among their employees. While some companies are creating a positive culture for employees to grow, discover, and learn, many companies are paying lip-service to learning and individual growth.

Fortunately, I have had the chance to work with CEOs, CFOs, or CHROs who believed learning, growth, and curiosity were not a cost but an investment. At the same time, I have personally observed many organizations stifling curiosity of new employees the very moment they join the company, companies minimally investing in training the employees just enough so they can do their current roles (and not prepare them for potentially next roles) and treating growth and development as non-productive time that should be avoided as much as possible.

A good example of an executive leader and role model for curiosity is Vas Narasimhan, the CEO of the pharmaceutical company Novartis. He ensured curiosity became an overarching corporate value for the company and worked with his CHRO and Simon Brown, the company's chief learning officer to "go big on curiosity." Simon Brown's aspirational target of one hundred hours of learning per person per year is encouraging employees to have a broad definition of learning, has democratized access of all available content to all employees (even if the content is not relevant for the employee's current role), and communicates regularly to employees the value of curiosity. Vas Narasimhan, clearly being a curious leader himself, acts as a role model for all to follow and underscores the importance of learning in his communication.

This kind of behavior at Novartis supports a trend we have been observing in recruitment: for young professionals learning and development opportunities trump salary in their decision to join the company of their choice. Added to this is a new mindset in the workforce: employees are looking for an organization where they can be their authentic selves. They are looking for companies with a clear organizational purpose, where they can grow toward mastery in their chosen fields and where they can go about their day job with as much autonomy as possible. They are looking for self-determination.

Another inspirational example is the airline engine company Pratt & Whitney. The vice president of their supply chain group, Jim Hamakiotis, introduced curiosity in his organization to empower employees and help the organization become more agile. To manage this culture transformation process, he hired Vincent-Pierre Giroux in early 2020, reporting directly to him. Since then, Mr. Giroux has been driving a culture transformation based on curiosity, first within the executive team before rolling it out across the organization. I can attest personally to the energy of Mr. Hamakiotis and the commitment of his entire management team as I was invited to address the team and talk about the power of workplace curiosity in early 2021.

Vincent-Pierre Giroux has embedded curiosity in leadership development programs and in team collaboration initiatives. Beyond L&D, he is using curiosity to redesign their offices for a post-COVID-19 hybrid reality and is using curiosity as an intentional lever to strengthen the company's diversity and inclusion agenda. What began with a humble start in their supply chain business is gradually finding its way to the broader organization, even its parent organization Raytheon.

While the C-suite decides on the budget, middle management defines the details of what the learning agenda is. Learning is decided by business management, not L&D and then pushed to the employees. This is done often without checking with employees whether they need this training or whether the organization benefits from this training.

The learning strategist Charles Jennings calls this the "conspiracy of convenience." Both the manager and L&D conspire in pretending they are doing something positive about developing their teams. The manager can say something is done and L&D is happy to comply, while deep down both realize nothing fundamental will change. Who has not done leadership training or sales training, only to realize one year later, the original problem to be tackled by the training is still rampant in the organization? In the next story, we will see an example where it is not middle management who sets the agenda, but the chief human resources officer who creates new space for learning.

CURIOSITY MINDSET TRAINING

Niklas Lindholm is chief HR officer of one of the oldest companies in the world: Fiskars. The company was founded in 1649 and has kept innovating all these years. In the HR and learning space, Niklas has also been innovating. One of the new developments he shared with me was they reframed how they approach leadership development. Instead of focusing on feeding concepts like strategy, operational excellence, or finance, to leaders, they are focusing now on building deeper self-awareness among their leaders.

What started as a program for their top 250 is now being rolled out across the organization to all employees. Other companies, like McKinsey & Company, have also been investing part of their L&D budgets to allow their employees to explore themselves at a more personal and deeper level and clarify questions like: What is my purpose? What are my values? What are my (limiting) beliefs?

Fiskars and McKinsey are good examples of companies going beyond teaching their employees in primary and secondary skills. Primary skills refer to the skills and knowledge supporting core business processes and secondary skills refer to skill and knowledge supporting individuals with their individual growth. Training in primary skills would cover topics related to supporting the core processes of the organization such as product or process training or for instance training to learn how to perform the current role (e.g., knowledge of how to write new code or operate a piece of machinery). Secondary skills training is training to help employees. It would be like training new employees business etiquette or teaching new managers the basics of people management or leaders on topics such as strategy.

This is where L&D teams in most companies typically draw the line. Some companies have been exploring with "tertiary" or meta-skills, i.e., skills to build individual and organizational future muscle. This is the realm where employees are invited to explore and improve their habits and mindsets like growth mindset, resilience, and curiosity. Given the increasing body of research and knowledge that mindsets like curiosity are trainable and not fixed, few L&D teams are looking at training these mindsets as the next frontier for L&D to tackle.

YIN AND YANG

When it comes to curiosity, there are two complementary philosophies. The first philosophy is grounded in the belief curiosity needs a conducive environment. If we ensure the right environment, employees will show up curiously. All efforts are focused on creating the right external conditions for the employee to learn faster and better. The second philosophy believes it is important for the company to proactively support the employee in embracing an individual curious mindset.

The first school has as object of attention the nurture side of the equation; the second school focuses on the nature side.

Merck KGaA, Darmstadt, Germany is a good example of this second approach. I introduced this company in the last chapter. The company adopted intentional curiosity as a strategic enabler since 2015. They have fully embraced workplace curiosity, having gone deep in the research and broad in the application of workplace curiosity. In terms of learning, they have been adopting the mindset that individual curiosity can be influenced positively.

As a focus of their attention, the company has designed curiosity activation training for both individuals and teams. Training has been centered around teams to become better at idea generation strategies, techniques to welcome new ideas in the group, and approaches to implement new ideas faster. Simple yet powerful techniques like encouraging employees to use the word "and" instead of "but" when replying to colleagues are introduced into teams.

Adrian Stäubli, global head talent development at Zurich Insurance Group, introduced me to another good example. At the suggestion of his team member Nina Wittmer, Nina and he created a network of "curiosity ambassadors" to help the company move its learning agility needle. Adrian Stäubli and Nina Wittmer were conscious with the changing focus of the company on improving the "sustainability of work" that the L&D strategy also needed to step up. Stepping up meant, among other things, improving the impact of learning, helping employees to navigate the large offering of training programs, and increasing the level of L&D related communication to employees around the world.

One of their special solutions to achieve this goal is to bring together a network of "curiosity ambassadors." They have tapped into the energy of 170 global colleagues outside of their department and engaged them around this common goal. The focus of the network is to act as role models for the organization. Mr. Stäubli and Ms. Wittmer provide the overall purpose of the community, guidance, and inspiration and the 170 curiosity ambassadors carry the message forward in their respective organizations with zest.

What is also remarkable about the Zurich Insurance Group case is an organization in the insurance space is embracing curiosity. The insurance business is typically risk-averse and traditionally values compliance more than curiosity. Mr. Stäubli shared with me that is intentional. They realize, although Zurich Insurance Group is in the business of managing risks toward customers, it does not mean there shouldn't be room for innovation. They are encouraging employees to explore new knowledge and skills and are proactively creating a group of role models to lead the way.

In my view, a dual focus is the best, one where there is equal focus on both the intrinsic as well as the extrinsic layer.

PepsiCo is also a good example of a dual approach. Soon after she joined in February 2019 as chief learning officer for PepsiCo, Molly Nagler and her team started exploring ways to create a curious environment for the PepsiCo employees. When doing a curiosity program with them, they shared they have partnered with the learning experience technology company Degreed to create a customer-grade experience. The platform also helps in recommending a variety of content-assets based on the employee's goals, allowing people to follow colleagues, creating personalized learning pathways, and sharing competency improvement progress.

Molly Nagler and her team are also beginning to approach curiosity as a skill able to be influenced, learned, and developed. They have been curating over one hundred resources for curiosity, from articles about its business value to how curiosity can strengthen your relationships. But they aren't stopping there. I have supported them in baselining their organizational curiosity within the PepsiCo university team as well as across the organization. This benchmark has given input to a dedicated team to work on a strategy to:

1. Develop curiosity prompts and exercises that can be used in team meetings in under fifteen minutes.

2. Create short-content modules that can be embedded in our existing leadership and management programs.

3. Record videos from senior leaders sharing mini case studies on the role of curiosity at work.

We spoke earlier about the difference between productive and unproductive curiosity. Productive curiosity starts with new questions, focus to reach an answer, and discipline throughout. Erin Gruwell is a good example of a secondary school teacher bursting with productive curiosity. Regardless of whether you focus first on creating a conducive environment or also focus on curiosity as a skill to be learned and developed, L&D has the opportunity to become the competitive differentiator for their organizations.

Why don't we stay on this topic of innovation for a bit longer and explore the relationship between workplace curiosity, corporate success, and marketing? What exactly is the influence of curiosity on marketing? I am sure you can already think of advertisements that piqued your curiosity. This will be the focus of the next chapter.

The Big Ideas

The burning platform and the case for change for the learning and development function is clear. Industries are changing at remarkable speeds; new employees are handpicking those organizations who are promoting curiosity and learning. Like the IT department thirty years ago, the learning and development department can reinvent itself to support the challenges facing their companies.

Some companies are responding to these challenges with ambition and curiosity; some prefer the status quo. Some are encouraged by their CEO to do better; some challenge themselves to do so, some don't. The challenge remains. It is not a question whether learning and development departments will change, it is when will they?

The strategic importance for L&D to be a change agent becomes clear with the following data. A survey of 1056 European knowledge workers by the Center of the Future of Work - Cognizant found most workers seem unaware that reskilling is important. A staggering 65 percent of them expressed confidence that their current skill set would carry them through their career. Many employees don't see the need or know what to learn or how to reskill themselves.

Often, they just don't have time to learn, reflect, and improve. In my own research of curiosity among leaders, 60 percent of middle managers indicate they have no time to learn new skills or to explore new ideas.

We can learn from the best practices. The traits of curious learning and development teams are they are not afraid to explore new approaches, question themselves, challenge their long-held beliefs, and work with their CEOs to drive impact. They are curious about the science of learning, about the changing role of their trade, about the individual success of each single employee, about the success of their company and its customers, and about the culture they can influence. They also specifically train the leaders and employees in their care on the concept of curiosity.

Questions for Reflection

- How is your company teaching employees to get better at mindsets such as curiosity?

- Is the L&D agenda in your company focusing on the individual and organizational learning? Why or why not?

- Are you tapping into the collective knowledge of your employees? Is every employee invited to share her/his knowledge across organizational boundaries?

- How much are you embedding curiosity in your corporate training programs (new employee onboarding, sales, leadership)? What would happen if you added more?

- When it comes to looking at L&D through the lens of curiosity, what would you advise your company to start, stop, or continue?

13

ROMAN HOLIDAY: CURIOUS ABOUT MARKETING AND SALES

———

*"It is astonishing how whole industries will display
a complete lack of marketing insight without
anyone in the industry thinking much is amiss."*

—WILLEM BURGERS, PROFESSOR OF

STRATEGY AND MARKETING

What makes the story of Gregory Peck and Audrey Hepburn
in the movie *Roman Holiday* so interesting for marketeers?
The story of this 1953 romantic comedy is lovely in its simplicity: it describes a bored and somewhat naïve princess
who sets out to spend a day incognito in Rome together with
an opportunistic reporter. When the reporter first meets
the princess, he initially is unaware of the real identity of
the royal. When he learns who she really is, he tries to have
her spend the day with him to catch a news story. During

the day, both become attracted to each other and out of his newfound love, he relinquishes the idea of writing a story. After twenty-four hours, they both return to their own worlds, cherishing the experience.

If you are interested in old black-and-white movies, you likely know this one. If you don't, you might have viewed the scene where they both visit the Mouth of Truth, the marble mask statue where Gregory Peck's character tricks the princess into thinking his hand has been bitten off.

Some people might even remember the scene where Audrey Hepburn learns to ride a Vespa motorcycle. Learning to ride a motorcycle might come across as a nice cinematographic idea. In 1953, this scene did more than meet the eye at the surface. This scene was an early example of product placement. In fact, the movie helped launch the Vespa scooter internationally. It was the biggest sales promotion for the scooter. Piaggio, the company behind Vespa, sold a record one hundred thousand scooters in 1952, the year *Roman Holiday* was released.

Another reason it helped sales was because a woman drove the Vespa, a novelty in those days. The special design of the Vespa enabled women wearing skirts to comfortably drive the motorcycle (Hinchliffe 2017).

Product placement is a method subliminally promoting brands and products to the consumer and, if done well, can help a brand increase its sales as in the Vespa example. It only requires curiosity, openness to finding new solutions on the part of the marketing team to come up with creative solutions. It also creates a desire in the mind of the consumer.

Another successful example is how product placement saved Ray-Ban. Ray-Ban was a struggling company, and its "Wayfarer" model was going nowhere. In 1982, they only sold eighteen thousand pairs. With their back to the wall, they experimented with a new marketing approach and teamed up with Tom Cruise to wear Wayfarers in his movie *Risky Business*. In 1983, the year the movie was released, as many as 360 thousand pairs were sold.

Remember, just two years earlier, only eighteen thousand were sold. In the 1986 movie *Top Gun*, Cruise again wore these sunglasses, leading to sales increasing another 40 percent. Because of smart marketing, Wayfarers soon became the sunglasses of choice for most Hollywood celebrities, increasing their popularity exponentially (Jurberg 2020).

The above examples are indicative of two marketing initiatives resulting in big successes for their companies. The marketeers in these companies explored new avenues to promote their product (or to save their business) and hit the proverbial gold mine. At the heart of these successes lies curiosity, which serves as the initial spark for creativity to be turned into action.

Another aspect of curiosity is its desire to explore the unknown and the readiness to potentially fail in the pursuit of success.

Curiosity is key for marketers as successful marketers embrace continuous experimentation. Nine out of ten ideas might not work. The one idea that works will always make up for the other nine failures. Marketing is no binary science, it is probabilistic and requires marketeers' willingness to explore the things they know, they don't know, and more importantly to explore the things they don't know they don't know. Really good marketeers are hard to come by. Companies should check for curiosity in their new (and current) hires. Marketing needs out-of-the-box thinkers; people who are not afraid to test, fail, and test again. Those companies that reward constant experimentation and celebrate the associated failures will thrive."

—Willem Burgers

INFORMATION GAP THEORY IN PRACTICE

Marketeers have structurally been adopting some concepts from psychology to arouse the curiosity of their customers, so they purchase the desired products. One proven technique advertisers use is to use the information gap concept in marketing. This concept builds on the natural curiosity of people: when presented with some partial information, people experience a negative sensation called an information gap. The normal reaction of curious people is to solve this gap by acquiring further information, for instance, by clicking an online link. The simplest version of the information gap is when one hears a knock on the door when one does not expect it. The sound of the knock makes us look up in the direction of the door and makes us walk over to the window to peek out to see who it is.

Teaser campaigns are a good example of this concept. A teaser campaign is an advertisement campaign typically consisting of a series of small, cryptic advertisements that anticipate a larger, full-blown campaign for a product launch or otherwise important event. We have all experienced emails titled: "something BIG is coming."

The Chinese electronics company Xiaomi came out with a teaser advertisement campaign to launch one of their new flagship smartphones in 2015. On a black background, we can imagine seeing in big white letters:

"As _____ as paper. Xiaomi new flagship launch. TWO DAYS TO GO."

Consumers interested who are already into the brand or who are looking to buy a new smartphone might be motivated to wait two days before making a buying decision. Not those potential customers have much to go by; literally nothing is disclosed in the ad about what this product might be, but Xiaomi clearly wants everyone to know what it isn't: thick, heavy, or mediocre.

Clickbait headlines invite readers into the same information gap trap. In a clickbait-style headline, the news platform Mother Jones got readers to click by writing a headline based on their fear: "The Scary New Science That Shows Milk Is Bad for You." The strategy they followed was if you drink milk, which many people do, reading this headline will make you feel afraid. You'll naturally want to click to find out more (Harkingson 2015).

Not knowing the reason why creates an information gap in the mind. Many people find themselves clicking on the link and continue reading the article to find out more. Interestingly, the milk article doesn't directly say milk is bad for you; instead, it talks about how adults don't need as much calcium as previously suggested.

What marketing experts have found is the information gap should not be too easy or too difficult. It should be about just right for people to take the plunge. There are two conditions that need to be met. People first need to have the feeling that the information at hand is interesting enough to pursue. In the case of the smartphone brand Xiaomi: I need to be interested in the brand Xiaomi in the first place and/or want to buy or upgrade my smartphone, otherwise I would disregard this information and focus on one of the other five thousand advertisements the average person is exposed to daily. Second, people need to be sure they have the means to close the gap. In the Xiaomi case, they need to have financial means to engage further.

Deep down, all advertisement is about creating a real or perceived need, a gap in the minds of customers. Advertisements try to trigger people into spending money to satisfy a craving sensation.

Advertisements can also kill curiosity. The more people see a message, the more they start to believe in them. The more they believe the brand or the carrier, the more they believe the message of the advert, even if the product is something we don't need or is harmful for our health. We all know the cigarette advertisements of the 1950s where a doctor is endorsing smoking. We also know cigarette companies were sponsoring such advertisements to counter the early messages that cigarette smoking was not good for one's health. This encouraged cigarette smokers not to inquire about the health issues associated with cigarette smoking.

I want to share a small tangential example of something that happened to me recently, an example about the danger of the internet.

I was reviewing some old advertisement campaigns from the 1950s in preparation for a keynote address for a marketing congress. I found the perfect caricature of a vintage advertisement: a Coca-Cola advertisement encouraging parents to have infants drink Coca-Cola under the slogan: "For a Better Start in Life, Start Cola Earlier." In the advert, this claim is supported by stating scientific proof that babies who drink soda have a much higher chance of being accepted and fitting in their peer group in their teens.

A perfect advert to make a point about information gap theory and to prove adverts can be downright misleading and discourage consumers to be curious themselves. I was picturing myself already sharing this example with the audience. A little voice in my head, however, suggested digging a bit deeper. To my horror, I found that this vintage ad was fake. It had never been commissioned by Coca-Cola. It was created in 2002 intentionally as a fake vintage ad (Jdryznar 2002).

Without an inquisitive curious mind, there is a chance we fall for such messages when we are exposed to them regularly and stop questioning their validity. We can laugh with such adverts from seventy years ago, not realizing print media has been replaced by recurring messages presented in our social media feeds trying to influence, even trick us with clickbait headlines.

GOOD VERSUS BAD MARKETING

There is something peculiar about the human psyche. On the one hand, we are internally a confirmation-seeking species, preferring a comfortable past and yet often avoid the uncertainty of an unknown future. This often reflects in our buying behavior. We stick often to the brands and products we know from the past, even when new, better, and cheaper products are available. For some products, however, we do the opposite and want to be associated with innovative companies, particularly when they are successful.

Apple is a good example. Instead of sticking with the same phone for a couple of years, a certain percentage of consumers can't wait to dump last year's model and replace it with the latest. Marketing has a big role to play in priming consumers to act in a slightly economically irrational way: why do we want to throw away a fully functional smartphone and invest the equivalent of often more than half a month's salary to replace it with a more expensive model? The same replacement behavior we seem to have with non-technology products.

The Swedish home decoration company IKEA has been promoting the same behavior. We ditch the blue sofa we bought last year and replace it with a red sofa this year, not because we need one, but because…we can. It's not really a choice driven from a mindset of sustainability and conservation of our precious resources. One must be in awe of the clever strategies marketing companies wield over consumers, especially in the face of recent focus on sustainability in companies.

I hope these marketing teams turn their focus on educating their consumers to be aware of their ecological footprint, while they still strive to make money for their companies.

I am confident the savvy marketers at Apple will be able to find a solution to this. The Apple marketing teams have—after all—been finding solutions to problems in places where nobody else was looking. Willem Burgers gave me a couple of telling examples. While all other MP3 brands were adding buttons to increase usability on their devices, Apple reframed their mental model and reversed this trend: they eliminated buttons. According to Professor Burgers, Steve Jobs' own exposure to Zen Buddhism might have influenced this thinking. "Zen Buddhism encourages the ultimate open mindset: if you ask about specifics and what a certain thing is, you actually have already asked too much. For Steve Jobs, this meant the ultimate computer was no computer in the strict sense of the word and could be designed based on simplicity."

Professor Burgers continued with another example: "While virtually all other brands were fine in going with black earbuds, marketeers at Apple were the first ones to go big on... white earbuds."

> All these companies had well-paid marketing executives, budgets, and teams, yet they all opted for status quo or at least did not explore the limits of their thinking. They might have had the idea of different earbud colors but did not act on these ideas. The people at Apple did have the ideas, had the environment which supported these ideas, and encouraged its implementation.

Exploring the things you don't know pays off more handsomely than looking for confirmation of the things you do know.

In the 1990s, Nokia asked a similar question: What if our consumers could change the cover of their phones, and what if they could personalize their ringtones? We don't think of this nowadays, as few of us keep the standard settings, yet in the early days of mobile telephony, this was revolutionary. Nokia is a good example of the need for continuous and intentional curiosity. It is not because you hit a homerun once that you can rest on your laurels. Marketing requires continuous experimentation.

Netflix is a good recent example of the power of curiosity in marketing and product management. Before online movie streaming became the de facto standard, Netflix started in the early movie rental business. They had, however, read the early signs of the promising potential of the internet. They had made experimentation part of their culture: Faced with competition from the much bigger company Blockbuster, they had experimented with DVD postal subscription. Before internet movie streaming existed, consumers had to visit movie rental shops. Netflix created a new service where people did not have to take the trip, but instead order the movies online. Netflix then posted the DVDs in the mail. This was an important step in eliminating the need for investments in brick-and-mortar rental outlets. In 2007, their founder and CEO, Reed Hastings, decided to transition from DVD shipments to online programming.

We all know well what happened afterward. What is less known is that in 2000, Mr. Hastings proposed a partnership to his much bigger competitor: Blockbuster. His proposal was a collaboration where Netflix would run Blockbuster's brand online while Blockbuster would promote Netflix in its stores. Blockbuster turned Netflix down. Goliath was not interested in sharing a potentially much bigger cake with David (Huddleston 2020).

In 2010, Blockbuster filed for bankruptcy. Netflix did not stop there and has gone on to become a world power in the movie business both downstream and upstream. It continued to innovate, creating its own production division, turning out, for instance, the successful *House of Cards* TV series. In 2012, Netflix spent a staggering seventeen billion US dollars on creating series and movies. In 2019, Netflix received fourteen Oscar nominations, winning four. This put Netflix on par with the other major studios for Academy Award wins.

LESSONS

I was interested in finding out why some companies are better at marketing than other companies, and why some marketers create magic and go places while others swim stationary. The UK-based online marketing consultant and curious thinking advocate Charlie Whyman helped me in formulating some of the challenges of marketers as well as potential lessons.

What is holding marketeers back is their lack of confidence to speak out in the organizational cultures they find themselves in. (She made the analogy with engineering.) In engineering, testing is designed to explore under which conditions the solution breaks down, then you improve until you get it right. In a lot of companies, marketing is afraid of failing and, therefore, afraid of testing.

Another reason for a diminished attention to curiosity in marketing, she thought, is work pressure. "Back-to-back meetings, juggling too many projects at the same time does not create the right atmosphere for marketeers to pause and think how they can do things better. To be creative, people need to be curious. To be curious, people need time and space to ask better questions." I agree with her. It is not so much about asking more questions. Rather, it is about asking better and more intentional questions.

For her, curiosity is not a nice-to-have; it is the required attitude to step back in order to jump farther: "We make a lot of assumptions in marketing. Curiosity makes us avoid assumptions and back them up with evidence and data, making marketeers more credible and more effective." She advised her technology sector customers to adopt minimum viable product (MVP) strategies. The company created a basic version and then invited their customer to co-create the next versions of their product together.

Ms. Whyman often uses her "OTTER" methodology when advising customers. "OTTER" stands for:

- **Objectives**: Ensure objectives of a new project or initiative are "smart" (specific, measurable, achievable, relevant, and time-bound). She also suggests teams add an element of constraint and challenge in the process. According to her: adding the right level of constraint challenges people's thought processes positively to come up with creative solutions to solve specific problems in a set timeframe.

- **Tools**: Explore tools to achieve the objectives. Tools include adopting a curious mindset and a strategy to explore asking better and novel question strategies.

- **Training**: Help bridge the gap between the status quo and the skills required by investigating gaps in skills, confidence, experience, and knowledge.

- **Expectations**: Get expectations right and realistic. How much time, money, and energy is the team expected to put into the objective? Teams are often not specific enough about their expectations, either they want too much, or they are not aligned with the rest of the organization and management.

- **Reflect and review**: Reflect on what can be done better. Sometimes this also means reflecting on what the team is doing well already and continuing this instead of jumping on a new trend.

CREATING CURIOUS SALES

Finding out customer expectations is ultimately an act of empathy. The more a sales representative is intrinsically interested in their customer, the more long-term relations and sales are generated.

Sales teams in companies are being educated to be better at listening, at learning better about the customers. When I worked at Royal Philips in the Netherlands, one of my teams was responsible for the sales and marketing learning and development processes. We launched a companywide program to educate our twelve thousand sales colleagues around the world to embrace what we called "customer-focused selling." We equipped them to go beyond product sales and provided them tools to intentionally empathize with their customer as well as ensure the customer needs were deeply understood well before there was a discussion about what solution to offer to the client. The solution did not have to be a product; it could be a service where Philips kept ownership of the product and leased it to the customer, or where there was a pay-per-use arrangement. Instead of buying a capital-intensive healthcare application like an MRI, customers had the option to buy the product, lease it with regular payments, or pay a use fee.

Interestingly, what we learned in the process was it was much more important to educate the managers than the salespeople. In our learning design, we had factored in management was also to receive a shorter version of the training program, simply to ensure they were familiar with the new language we introduced to sales. (In the management sessions, we also introduced leaders to new ways of reading advanced CRM data to help them with better sales forecasting, manage customer throughput, and deal velocity.) Yet early in the launch, we had the opportunity to tag along with a global sales management meeting for a division. As a trial, we trained the sales managers in the new sales methodology and provided them with tools to introduce these concepts to their sales teams. The sales teams were only introduced to a half-day session instead of the three-day workshop we were rolling out elsewhere.

What was remarkable was the adoption rate of the new concepts was remarkably higher for the group where we had done more with the managers and less with the sales reps. The reason for this is simple: people respond to the expectations of the leader. If the subordinates are trained without the manager's knowledge, she (the manager) will not lead the team toward new expected behavior. If, however, the manager is triggered to change, then she will ensure the team follows, even if the team does not fully know the underlying logic.

Another dimension to the program was we had selected one to three of our best sales reps to train these concepts to others and mentor their peers in the quarters following the initial session to ensure deep embedding. The only requirements were that they had to be respected as being proven sales professionals, had the backing of local management, and were themselves motivated to move into a temporary new role. The course feedback from participants was more than 30 percent higher than the external facilitators we had hired.

Let's change the pace a bit. We have explored the drivers of curiosity, who the main actors are, and how various organizational disciplines approach curiosity. I am sure you have had some ideas already about how you can become even more curious. That's what the next chapter will be all about.

The Big Ideas

Curiosity is the foundation of creativity in marketing as well as success in customer sales. Those companies that enable the environmental factors of curiosity, such as providing time and space for reflection and encouraging experimentation, have a greater chance of outshining their competition.

Workplace curiosity in a marketing or sales setting is not simply being open-minded. It is about being open to what we know and what we don't know and being humbly mindful to explore what is missing; then do something about it. It is about creating a culture of openness, including openness to failure, and posing open questions to customers or clients as opposed to closed yes/no questions. Better even, a celebration of failure. Companies like Inuit and Tata hand out prizes for workplace failures to teams and individuals.

Curiosity is equally about allowing marketing and sales teams (as well as the rest of the organization) time and space to be curious. Curiosity is a process, too, and you must allow people time to go through it.

It helps us to ask better questions. To quote Charlie Whyman: "It is not about asking more questions, it is about marketeers asking the right question and being intentional with their questions." Asking better questions presumes people have time and space to be curious.

Questions for Reflection

- How curious is your corporate marketing?

- What is the single best question marketing (or sales) should be asking?

- Is sales approached as a transactional activity or one where you need to be curious about your customer environment?

- Do people in marketing—and in other parts of the organization—have time and space to be curious?

- What would you advise your marketing (or sales) team to start/stop/continue?

.

PART FOUR

ARCHITECTING CURIOSITY

14

DESIGNING STRATEGIES TO GET (EVEN) BETTER AT CURIOSITY

———

"Twenty years from now you will be more disappointed by the things that you didn't do than the ones you did. So throw off the bowlines. Sail away from the safe harbor. Catch the trade winds in your sails. Explore. Dream. Discover."

—MARK TWAIN

How do I get better at curiosity? How does my team show up more curiously? What can we improve in our underlying organizational fabric to get better at curiosity?

I am convinced you have been asking yourself these questions throughout the book. We have established together that the benefits of curiosity are plenty. Curious professionals are happier in life, make faster careers, have better relationships, and are readier to welcome change and challenges. Curious leaders are more respected and better at optimizing current operations as well as introducing change into their teams. They are also more in tune with their own inner selves.

The A-players among us are naturally good at all aspects of curiosity, yet others need some support to rekindle their curiosity flame. B-players deep down want to be curious, yet several factors have led to a diminished capacity. Stress, anxiety, years of routine, overconfidence, a lack of role models, and a stifling corporate culture all have contributed to what prevents B-players from showing up curiously at work.

It does not have to be this way. We have seen that curiosity is part trait, part state. It is partly fixed; the other part, however, is malleable and can be strengthened.

We have also seen that there are many dimensions to curiosity:

- Empathic/intellectual/self-reflective
- Broad versus narrow
- Productive versus unproductive
- Intrinsic versus extrinsic
- And more

The challenge we all face is where to start.

In this chapter, I share some proven strategies to kickstart your curiosity journey. They can be used at a level of individual, team, or organization. I encourage you to explore them and reflect on how you can apply them to your own situation and workplace.

STRATEGY 1: BE SERIOUS ABOUT CURIOSITY

Being serious and proactive about your interest in the world and the people around you and exploring your inner self will invariably bring more positive results compared to a reactive mindset or leaving things to chance. Develop a habit of curiosity. Put a reminder in your calendar or smartphone to allow time for curiosity, learning new things, and meeting people. Picture yourself as someone who values curiosity, learning, mental flexibility, and searching for knowledge. Tell yourself that from now on, you want to initiate a new transformation, one of intentional curiosity.

If you are leading a team or an organization, put curiosity on the team agenda. I mean this literally. Reserve about 25 percent of your weekly meeting time named "curiosity" and invite the team to share curious facts and come up with new ideas. Allow them to open up to ideas. Don't judge. Make sure every single person is heard.

Adopting this approach might feel a bit strange at first, yet my experience is when you persist, after a couple of rounds, the team will cherish these moments. It's best to start the meeting with this agenda point. It will prime the team to be more open to creative solutioning and empathic listening throughout the entire meeting.

Proactivity can take many forms. As individuals, we can actively influence our curiosity muscle and create transparency by taking a curiosity diagnostic and getting insights on our own curiosity. Once we know the direction of where we want to invest more of our time and energy, our proactivity will always pay off.

Companies can also be proactive in a myriad of ways. In 2014, when Satya Nadella became CEO of Microsoft, his first step was to change the culture of his company from a know-it-all to a learn-it-all environment. He not only encouraged himself to be proactively curious and adopt a growth mindset, but he also invited his entire organization to follow in his footsteps.

It is clear by now you are willing to embrace change. It is simple; if you weren't, you would not be exploring this chapter. To me, you have already won.

STRATEGY 2: APPROACH CURIOSITY AS A PROJECT

There are several logical steps professionals, teams, and organizations can take to engage in a journey to get (even) better at curiosity.

- Reflect on your definition of curiosity
- Measure
- Create strategies to improve
- Embed new practices in your routines
- Celebrate and influence

Regardless of whether you are an individual or a team, what is important with this specific strategy is treating curiosity as a project. A project has a well-defined idea of what the issue is, what is to change, and by when. There is a clear understanding about the baseline, where we are now, a deadline for when we will have changed, a plan of how to get there, outcome measures, and some resources.

If you are an individual, you might decide yourself how to grow your curiosity muscle. My experience is it is useful to get support from a trusted colleague. This support can be informal and limited to asking the person to give feedback on our own behavior in the group. This support can also be more formal. In that case, regular mentoring sessions can help. I have also seen the successful engagement of a personal coach who helped in keeping track of the objectives of the project.

At the team level, the leader herself will likely be the project leader. At an organizational level, a dedicated project manager is the best recipe for success. In this regard, we discussed Christine Blum-Heuser of Merck KGaA, Darmstadt, Germany, and Vincent-Pierre Giroux of Pratt & Whitney as examples. Their success in adopting workplace curiosity is in no small way attributable to their focus and energy.

STRATEGY 3: STRENGTHEN YOUR AWARENESS

Build your capacity to become aware of your level of curiosity. Take time to take a step back and observe your own behavior. Become aware of the deeper drivers of your behavior. Know when you are showing up curiously and when you are not. Become conscious of the deeper patterns in life; especially explore the extremes and look for the deeper reasons of joy or sadness, resilience or stress, conformity or curiosity.

Ask yourself: "Why is my reaction to that situation or that person such?" "What does this say about me, my values, and how I show up in life in general?"

This is not always easy. We assume we are always rational agents. We are not. Even finding a partner is sensitive to drivers we are not aware of. Research shows finding the ideal partner with dating in the evening is more difficult for us than, for instance, early morning. In the evening, our minds are often so full after a day's work, we have less capacity to see the people in front of us clearly for who they are. It would be, therefore, better to date people for breakfast. Daniel Kahneman in his 2011 book *Thinking Fast and Slow* shares many similar examples, such as highly educated parole officers being less likely to grant parole to inmates when they are hungry.

How aware are you of your conscious and unconscious drivers at work and at home?

Try to become aware of your values and beliefs, even your limiting beliefs and biases. The better you can articulate them, the easier it is for you to stand firm in your strength and to realize when you are residing in a place of conformity, routine, or perhaps stress.

The more stress you have, the more incapable you are of being curious. The more you can understand what creates stress for you at work and in life, the more you can create the necessary strategies to deal with the root causes of your stress. Fighting stress with curiosity can buffer you from vulnerabilities that can lead to depression and anxiety.

If you are a leader, ask yourself:

- Am I building openness in the team to allow for diverging points of view?

- Am I sensitive to groupthink? Am I creating a safe environment in the team where the individual members ask questions or challenge the strongest voice, or do I prefer that team members instead follow my decision, even if it is a bad one?

- Am I aware of my own reaction to suggestions from the team?

- Am I listening with an intent to learn or with an intent to convert people to my own point of view?

- Do I prefer the team to be curious or compliant?

- Am I driving the team toward exploitation, exploration, or (ideally) both? What does it say about me as a person and as a leader?

Don't confuse confidence with competence. We are often more critical of the competence of others versus rationally analyzing our own levels of expertise. Over 95 percent of professionals think they are better than others (Goldsmith 2007). The better you think you are, the greater the risk you're overestimating yourself—and the greater the odds you will stop improving. Hubris leads to downfall. The right dose of humility, the acceptance there is always more to learn, helps against arrogance.

Remember we discussed the difference between narrow and broad curiosity? Narrow curiosity is the type of curiosity that builds on our expertise and leads to deepening of our existing knowledge base. We need narrow curiosity to become better at our core skills. Broad curiosity allows us to explore new terrains and learn new skills. Broad curiosity allows us to be comfortable in being a constant novice while exploring new and unfamiliar terrains. Curious people need both: going deep and going broad.

I encourage you to reflect on your own curiosity patterns. Do you focus your curiosity on staying in tune with the development in your own area of expertise or are you interested in learning beyond your known world?

If your answer is both, how do you divide your exploration across these two percentagewise?

STRATEGY 4: MAKE YOUR CURIOSITY TRANSPARENT

The more you measure, the more you can take intentional action. The good thing is curiosity can be measured whether it is intrinsic individual or extrinsic organizational curiosity. Doing such assessments has multiple values. It helps as a map to explore the different dimensions of curiosity and it creates a baseline.

In my work with leaders, I regularly receive feedback from clients regarding the individual curiosity diagnostic my institute provides at no charge. These leaders share the following: not only does it help expose them to a new dimension of themselves, but it also expands their definition of curiosity.

Many tell me they are thinking of curiosity with the external world as its object of interest, not considering one also can be curious about what is going on inside them.

Once curiosity has been made transparent, a deeper level of analysis can begin. Do I (for individuals) or we (for teams) recognize these data? Do they resonate? What can I/we learn from this? Am I/Are we happy with these results, or how can they be improved?

I have worked with teams and organizations where the culture of conformity was so high, curiosity was considered a menace. Some companies are overly focused on adherence to conformity processes. Having people challenge the status quo is bad for business and could hurt business, safety, and customer relationships. Exploitation and compliance in these companies is seen as positive. Exploration and curiosity are not.

What these groups have realized is, even in such rigid environments, there is room for curiosity and improvement. There is a need to be aware of the underlying rationale and to be constantly curious enough to ask the questions: How are our current processes still relevant, and how can we improve things?

Once companies have set a baseline, it is possible to measure trends over time.

STRATEGY 5: START SMALL

Start small. Whatever small means for you, start with yourself, the group of friends you regularly hang out with at work, your team, your department, or your management team.

Former colleague and now *Tiny Habits®* certified expert, Teena George introduced me to the world of habit reengineering. She shared,

> When you want to be more of something, a good practice to follow is to make it a habit. Habits, while often overlooked, are powerful in helping us make something a part of our identity. When trying to create habits, a good way to start is to start tiny. This is where BJ Fogg, founder of the Behavior Design Lab at Stanford and *Tiny Habits: The Small Changes that Change Everything*, comes in.

Dr. Fogg has researched a recipe for creating new habits. It has three elements: an anchor, a behavior, and a celebration. It goes this way:

- An **anchor** moment—an existing event/routine that you already do which will serve as your reminder to do the new behavior.

- New tiny **behavior**—this is a simple, scaled-back version of the new behavior.

- Instant **celebration**—a mindful moment where you reward yourself mentally.

For example, if you want to become more intentional about your curiosity, one thing you can start with is thinking of the following strategy:

When I find myself not knowing or understanding a term or concept in a meeting, I intentionally will want to grasp its meaning.

To do this, you could choose a meeting as your anchor moment. The tiny behavior could be writing down unfamiliar terms during the meeting and doing an online search immediately after the meeting. Alternatively, you can also step in your courageous shoes, tell the people in the meeting that you don't understand, and ask them to explain. Once you have accomplished either of these activities, you celebrate by giving yourself a pat on the back and telling yourself, "Good job."

Your *Tiny Habits*® recipe will look something like this—

Anchor—During the meeting when I encounter a concept I am not familiar with.

Behavior—I will (1) look it up after the meeting or (2) ask people to explain.

Celebration—Tell myself "good job" for getting started on the path to curiosity.

I recommend you get curious and creative for yourself by following the above recipe. By creating them and putting them into practice, you will be well on your way to becoming more curious.

In teams or organizations, start small too. Focus on one team or one department for starters, build momentum, and go from there. I had the pleasure of working with smaller and bigger teams. What they all have in common is a curious leader who is willing to take steps to embrace workplace curiosity as a force to make things better.

STRATEGY 6: DEVELOP YOURSELF AND OTHERS

Once you know what aspect of curiosity you want to get better at, you can start your journey. Part of the journey will be to collect more information. If you want to become better at self-reflective curiosity, you might want to get some inspiration by reading books or articles, discussing the topic with people you trust, or exploring some strategies like meditation.

Curiosity means to try something new, to learn something new, to nudge the edge of your comfort zone and introduce variety. It also means to do something positively unpredictable and exciting. Endeavor to preserve the ability to be surprised and to surprise others. Allow yourself to be surprised by serendipity. Set up a call with a colleague you normally don't talk to. If you are used to red wine, try to go for the white wine. Enter a bookstore and buy the book (or magazine) next to the one you want to buy; alternatively, choose a book from a section you're not familiar with or buy magazines on a topic completely new to you. If you always take the same route to work, try another one.

If you want to train others, let me share the following personal experience. For the last fifteen years or so, I have become interested in the concept of mindsets and the methods regarding how people can change to improve them. I was exposed to one of the earlier research projects on teaching growth mindset in secondary schools in the USA and other countries like China (Bedford 2017; Guang 2016).

The research showed, in a secondary school setting, academic performance of students could improve if these students were invited to self-reflect about their own mindsets and behaviors.

This was achieved by introducing students to the concept of neuroplasticity (i.e., the brain has the capability to change) by providing them concepts and metaphors to reflect on their own mindset and behavior and inviting them to share these concepts with other students.

Given this research had not been replicated for curiosity and working professionals, I was interested whether this would still be beneficial in another setting and for an older demographic.

What started as a small training pilot quickly grew into an extended pilot involving fifteen thousand professionals. The program seemed to strike a positive nerve in people in my organization. We checked back in with all course participants three months afterward to ask them a couple of follow-up questions. It was remarkable to see 52 percent indicated they were looking differently at the world versus prior to the session.

Sometime later, my team and I reviewed the learning hours of these people. We found twelve months prior to these sessions this group had on average consumed twenty-five hours of learning. In the twelve months after these sessions, learning consumption rose to a staggering forty-three hours.

We were on to something.

This was the single biggest reason why I left a cushy job and decided to set up the Global Curiosity Institute.

I have built on this experience and fine-tuned the process. Prior to sessions I deliver, I invite participants to self-assess their curiosity profile via a custom-made diagnostic.

An individual report outlining the participant's intellectual, empathic, and self-reflective curiosity is shared with each person.

What I have noticed is the reflection journey of the multifaceted nature of curiosity often starts from the moment of receiving the individual report. Post workshop, I invite participants to share the concept presented in the workshop to their team. This works especially well when delivering the program to leaders as they involve their teams in the concept of curiosity.

STRATEGY 7: BUILD NEW KNOWLEDGE, CONSTANTLY

Curiosity needs knowledge to build on and the more knowledge one possesses, the more curiosity is triggered. The more you engage in continuous learning—both in learning within your area of expertise and learning more broadly—the more you can ask fresh questions and come up with novel answers. On the other hand, the less one knows, the less questions he or she will ask.

The more people read, engage in intellectual debate, and learn, the more curiosity shows up.

> "To get a good idea, you must first get a lot of ideas."
>
> —THOMAS EDISON

The only way to get a lot of ideas is to be inspired by lots of knowledge.

Microsoft's founder, Bill Gates, is known to be an avid reader. In an interview, he shared the advantage of reading: "When you have a broad framework, then you have a place to put everything." Mr. Gates advocates exploring broadly when learning about things. "If you want to learn science, read the history of science and the story of scientists, find out when they were confused, what tools and insights allowed them to make the progress they made." According to him, this approach creates a mental map. The more one reads, the more detailed the map becomes and the easier new questions flow (Quartz 2019).

Constant learning is also a good antidote to retaining a healthy dose of humility that there is always more to learn, we are not right all the time, and we can always get better. The urge for knowledge also drives us to doublecheck right from wrong in the press and social media. It drives us to explore the messages we receive and test their validity.

In a team setting, we often refer to this validation—or the lack of it—as confirmation bias. The team (or the leader) is only willing to entertain ideas and suggestions which confirm their view of the world. As a result, all suggestions which don't conform get thrown out the window, even if they are correct.

You can fight confirmation bias, burst filter bubbles, and escape self-imposed echo chambers by actively learning about and engaging with ideas that challenge your assumptions. An easy place to start is following people who make you think differently, even if you usually disagree with what they think.

STRATEGY 8: QUESTION YOUR TEASPOONS

The phrase "question your teaspoons" was coined by the French writer Georges Perec. It is a perfect strategy to get better at curiosity. If you cannot be curious about the small and mundane things and tasks in life, you will have a harder time in being curious about the things that matter.

What we need to question is bricks, concrete, glass, our table manners, our utensils, our tools, the way we spend our time, our rhythms. To question that which seems to have ceased forever to astonish us. We live, true, we breathe, true; we walk, we open doors, we go down staircases, we sit at a table in order to eat, we lie down on a bed in order to sleep. How? Why? Where? When? Why?

Describe your street. Describe another street. Compare.

Make an inventory of your pockets, of your bag. Ask yourself about the provenance, the use, what will become of each of the objects you take out.

Question your teaspoons.

What is there under your wallpaper?

How many movements does it take to dial a phone number?

Why don't you find cigarettes in grocery stores? Why not?

It matters little to me that these questions should be fragmentary, barely indicative of a method, at most of a project. It matters a lot to me that they should seem trivial and futile: that's exactly what makes them just as essential, if not more so, as all the other questions by which we've tried in vain to lay hold on our truth (Nova 2008).

Questioning the obvious is hard, as we often do not notice it anymore. The routine and practice of years has made us blind to them. Yet doing so remains important. Every time someone new arrives on the scene, there is an opportunity to question the old realities again and ask: Why do we do things like this around here? Is there a better way?

If you just accept the world as it is without trying to dig deeper, you will certainly not discover everything you could explore. Never take things for granted.

STRATEGY 9: STRENGTHEN YOUR RELATIONSHIPS

Recognition and appreciation of the people you live and work with lead to better relationships. Instead of taking things for granted in your social lives, engage more actively with others. The more you actively engage with others with a curious and exploration mindset, the deeper lasting relationships you will forge.

I have shared earlier Professor Todd Kashdan's finding that most couples don't separate because they fight but because they are bored with each other. Bored couples take each other for granted, they stopped exploring, they are not interested in each other anymore.

Ditto in the workspace.

We might be interested in how a handful of people spent their weekend, yet how much do we really know about the people we work with daily on a deeper level?

In a workshop I did with a team, I invited colleagues to talk to each other by making the following statement and asking the following question:

1. (Statement) I respect you because…

2. (Question) What is something I don't know yet about you?

While many of these people had been working together for years, they had not taken the time to articulate what they respected in each other or learn to know their colleagues at a deeper level.

I encourage you to strengthen your relationships in the workplace, especially with those colleagues you do not talk to often. Try to make it a habit to talk to an old or new colleague on a (bi)weekly basis. Strive to connect with people with different points of view to yours and seek to understand their logic. Set out to meet people beyond your immediate circle. If you are in a customer interfacing role, aim to connect with more people in your client organization.

STRATEGY 10: EMBRACE FAILURE

Instead of avoiding failure at all costs, embrace when it arises as an opportunity to learn. There is no individual or organizational growth without it. Celebrate failures. Fail fast and small and learn fast.

One strategy could be to erase the word "mistake" from the individual or corporate vernacular. Edward Hess, professor emeritus of business administration at the Darden School of Business, shared a paradigm moment at the company Intuit Inc. when they decided to become more innovation minded. In Professor Hess' own words: "The Intuit leadership decided the word 'mistake' should no longer be used in their company. From then onward, they referred to things of that nature as 'surprise.' A surprise is good."

To conclude in Ralph Waldo Emerson's words:

> Don't be too timid and squeamish about your actions. All life is an experiment. The more experiments you make, the better. What if they are a little coarse and you may get your coat soiled or torn? What if you do fail, and get fairly rolled in the dirt once or twice? Up again, you shall never be so afraid of a tumble.

TEN STRATEGIES TO GET (EVEN) BETTER AT CURIOSITY

1. Be Serious about Curiosity
2. Approach Curiosity as a Project
3. Strengthen Your Awareness
4. Make Your Curiosity Transparent
5. Start Small
6. Develop Yourself and Others
7. Build New Knowledge, Constantly
8. Question Your Teaspoons
9. Strengthen Your Relationships
10. Embrace Failure

15

CONCLUSION

———

"By replacing the fear of the unknown with curiosity, we open ourselves up to an infinite stream of possibility."
—ALAN WATTS, PHILOSOPHER

How do you deal with curiosity? Are you embracing it or are you leaving it untouched? Are you encouraging others to also be curious?

This book is a manifesto, and as such, a call to action. The future will tell.

Curiosity is here to stay in this century of ideas. I agree with Ulrik Juul Christenssen, the CEO of the tech company Area9, when he asserts it is time we reverse the adage "curiosity killed the cat" and turn it into "incuriosity killed the cat." The world belongs to the curious.

In my family, we have a rule. We take time to eat together at a round dining table. My wife and I bought the table when our four children were still young. It can sit two people, yet it also easily sits twelve.

We have carried this table around the world. I don't know if it is the genie of the table, but next to eating, we also debate, discuss, and share our experiences, ideas, and thoughts at the table.

When we are together, everybody has an equal position at the table and also an equal voice. I believe this table has been one of the tools that keep curiosity growing and flowing at our home. It is also the table where I wrote a large part of the manuscript for this book.

How often do we take time to discuss important things at work?

There is one thing we can all agree upon: If a system cannot adapt, it cannot survive. If the environment changes, we need to adapt.

What we can also agree upon is: The fruits of our curiosity, learning, and openness will make both the present and the future better. Equipped with the right dose of curiosity, you will survive challenging situations and lead happy and profitable lives.

We don't have to start from scratch. Curiosity is part of our nature; we are all intrinsically good at it. We all have curiosity hardwired in us from birth. I referred earlier to the concept of curiosity as a muscle. The more we use it, the bigger and stronger it gets. Without intentional practice, or if we stop using it, it atrophies, becomes weak, and is prone to damage. With the right insight about how to change, a little discipline, and focus, we can all learn to become A-players.

Teams and organizations can also make changes to the way they manage the operations and their people and thus invite curiosity in.

Stress and routine have a way of diminishing our curiosity. We have a predisposition to conformity. Conformity to predictable and stable routines gives us peace of mind. The moments we are devoid of stress, we become open to novelty and are ready to let go of some of our routines.

Another metaphor to consider for curiosity is one of an investment into our bank account. The more curious we are, the more we are investing in our intelligence and knowledge, in our relationships, and in ourselves. When we expand our curiosity, we are linking disparate ideas together in new ways that were impossible until now. Alternatively, we find solutions to problems that did not bear fruit so far. The best investments are those that generate results in the long term.

The challenge is to overcome the comfortable pull from conformity. We create routines and narratives to give structure to our lives. Disrupting old routines and things we take for granted takes effort. A little bit of effort makes us explore the world we know more. More effort leads to the discovery of completely new territories.

Companies who create curious environments and are intentional about building conducive cultures, processes, and practices will thrive. They will attract the best talent and create a climate of confident humility, one where there is time and space for exploration. We have explored many examples together; I recommend you reflect on them: PepsiCo, Microsoft, Novartis, Zurich, Google, Quick Release, Area9, and many more.

Now it is time for you to add your example to the list or to start thinking about how you create a better version of yourself and your workspace.

They say curiosity is contagious. Let's start a movement together.

If you need help, visit www.globalcuriosityinstitute.com, where you will find a variety of resources, bonus chapters, tools, and tips to set you on the right path. You will find a curiosity diagnostic you can take and get a report of your own curiosity profile.

I'd love to stay in contact. I am curious about your evolving story. Drop me a note at stefaan@globalcuriosityinstitute.com if you want to talk.

BIBLIOGRAPHY

___

INTRODUCTION

Luo Mengyu Annie, Jiaojiao Li, and Jessica Boccardo. "New Vision for Education." Switzerland: World Economic Forum, March 2016. https://www3.weforum.org/docs/WEF_New_Vision_for_Education.pdf.

PART 1

CHAPTER 1

Anonymous. "Na acht weken zonder drank zien mensen er stukken beter uit." De Morgen, December 27, 2021.

Benstead, Sam (creator). 2020. *Babies*. Volume 1, part 2. *What Babies Know*. Accessed January 7, 2022. Netflix.

Burgers Willem. 2008. *Marketing Revealed: Challenging the Myths*. New York: Palgrave MacMillan.

Cambridge Dictionary Online, sv. "Curiosity." Accessed May 12, 2021. https://dictionary.cambridge.org/dictionary/english/curiosity.

Dobbs, David. "Teenage Brains." *National Geographic Magazine*. October 2011. https://www.nationalgeographic.com/magazine/article/beautiful-brains.

Gupta, Anil K., Ken G. Smith, Christina E. Shalley. "The Interplay Between Exploration and Exploitation." *Academy of Management Journal*. Vol. 49, No 4 (2006): 693-706. https://www.jstor.org/stable/20159793.

Leslie, Ian. 2014. *Curious: The Desire to Know and Why Your Future Depends on It*. London: Quercus Publishing Ltd.

Livio, Mario. 2017. *Why: What Makes Us Curious.* New York: Simon & Schuster Paperbacks.

Orwell, George. 1950. *1984.* New York: Signet Classic.

Steingold, Daniel. "Are We There Yet?' Children Ask Parents 73 Questions a Day on Average, Study Finds." Studyfinds. December 11, 2017. https://www.studyfinds.org/children-parents-questions/.

Webster, Joanne P., Maya Kaushik, Greg C. Bristow, and Glenn A. McConkey. "Toxoplasma Gondii Infection, From Predation to Schizophrenia?" *Journal of Experimental Biology,* January 1, 2013; 216(1): 99–112. https://www.ncbi.nlm.nih.gov/pmc/articles/PMC3515034/.

CHAPTER 2

Boynton, Andy, Bill Fisher. 2005. *Virtuoso Teams: The Extraordinary Stories of Extraordinary Teams.* Harlow: Pearson Education Limited.

Dobbs, David. "Restless Genes." *National Geographic Magazine.* January 2013. https://www.nationalgeographic.com/magazine/article/restless-genes.

Epstein, David. 2019. *Range: Why Generalists Triumph in a Specialized World.* New York: Riverhead Books.

Fry Stephen. 2010. *The Fry Chronicles: An Autobiography,* Cambridge: Michael Joseph. Quoted in: Leslie Ian. 2014. *Curious: The Desire to Know and Why Your Future Depends on It.* London: Quercus Publishing Ltd.

Gehricke Jean-G, James Swanson, Sophie Duang, Jenny Nguyen, Timothy Wigal, James Fallon, Cyrus Caburian, L. Tugan Muftuler, and Robert Moyzis. "Increased Brain Activity to Unpleasant Stimuli in Individuals with the 7R Allele of the DRD4 Gene." Psychiatry Res. January 30, 2015; 231 (1): 58–63. https://www.ncbi.nlm.nih.gov/pmc/articles/PMC4272659/.

Goldsmith, Marshall and Mark. Reiter. 2007. *What Got You Here Won't Get You There: How Successful People Become Even More Successful.* New York City: Hyperion.

Harrison Spencer. "Your Super Power Curiosity." April 29, 2021. In *The Curious Advantage Podcast,* Produced by Paul Ashcroft, Simon Brown and Garrick Jones. https://podcasts.apple.com/cz/podcast/your-superpower-curiosity-the-curious-advantage-podcast/id1509018267?i=1000519222390.

Jobs, Steven. Commencement Address at Stanford University. June 12, 2005. https://news.stanford.edu/2005/06/14/jobs-061505/.

Kashdan Todd B., David Disabato, Fallon Goodman, and Patrick McKnight. "The Five-Dimensional Curiosity Scale Revised (5DCR): Briefer Subscales While Separating Overt and Covert Social Curiosity." *Personality and Individual Differences,* April 2020. https://doi.org/10.1016/j.paid.2020.109836.

Kruger, Justin, and David Dunning. "Unskilled and Unaware of It." *Journal of Personality and Social Psychology.* Vol. 77. No. 6(2000). 1121–1134.

Loewenstein, George. "The Psychology of Curiosity: A Review and Reinterpretation." *Psychological Bulletin.* 1994. *Vol. 116. No. 1. 75–98.*

Rumsfeld, Donald. Press Conference by US Secretary of Defense. Brussels: NATO HQ, June 6, 2002.
https://www.nato.int/docu/speech/2002/s020606g.htm.

Tellegen Auke, David T. Lykken, Thomas J. Bouchard, Jr., Kimberly J. Wilcox, Nancy L. Segal, and Stephen Rich. "Personality Similarity in Twins Reared Apart and Together." *Journal of Personality and Social Psychology.* Vol. 54, No. 6 (1988). 1031–1039.
http://dx.doi.org/10.1037/0022-3514.54.6.1031.

Thorén, Pia-Maria. "What Is T-shaped Competence?" *Cornerstone Resource Corner Blog* (blog), March 1, 2019.
https://www.cornerstoneondemand.com/nl/resources/article/blog-what-is-t-shaped-competence-en-uk/.

Tsugawa, Yusuge. Daniel M. Blumenthal, Joseph P. Newhouse, Alan M. Zaslavsky, Anupam B. Jena. "Do Doctors Get Older as They Get Older?" *Harvard Business Review,* May 23, 2017.
https://hbr.org/2017/05/do-doctors-get-worse-as-they-get-older.

CHAPTER 3

Bebchuk, Lucian and Roberto Tallarita. "Was the Business Roundtable Statement Mostly for Show?" Harvard Law School Forum on Corporate Governance. August 18, 2020.
https://corpgov.law.harvard.edu/2020/08/18/was-the-business-roundtable-statement-mostly-for-show-2-evidence-from-corporate-governance-guidelines/.

Bhattacharya, Arindam, Nikolaus Lang, and Jim Hemerling. 2020. *Beyond Great: Nine Strategies for Thriving in an Era of Social Tension, Economic Nationalism and Technological Revolution.* London: Nicolas Brealey Publishing.

Business Roundtable. "Business Roundtable Redefines the Purpose of a Corporation to Promote 'An Economy That Serves All Americans.'" August 19, 2019.
https://www.businessroundtable.org/business-roundtable-redefines-the-purpose-of-a-corporation-to-promote-an-economy-that-serves-all-americans.

Garelli, Stéphane. "Why You Will Probably Live Longer than Most Big Companies." IMD Research and Knowledge Articles. December 2016.
https://www.imd.org/research-knowledge/articles/why-you-will-probably-live-longer-than-most-big-companies/.

Gino, Francesca. "The Business Case for Curiosity." *Harvard Business Review,* September 2018.
https://hbr.org/2018/09/the-business-case-for-curiosity.

Yestobeatrice. *George Eastman "The Wizard of Photography" Documentary* (Part 3/3)." July 21, 2015. YouTube Video, 17:54. https://www.youtube.com/watch?v=RwwWO6iqkUg.

Taleb, Nassim Nicholas. 2007. *The Black Swan: The Impact of the Highly Improbable.* New York: Random House.

Toffler, Alvin. 1970. *Future Shock.* New York: Random House.

CHAPTER 4

Berlyne, E.D. "A Theory of Human Curiosity." *British Journal of Psychology,* Vol. 45, No. 3 (August 1954). page 180.

Byrne, John A., William C. Symonds, Julia F. Siler, Karen Miller Lowry. "CEO Disease: Egotism Can Breed Corporate Disaster and the Malady Is Spreading." *Business Week,* April 1, 1991.

Edmondson, Amy C. 2018. *The Fearless Organization.* New York, NY: John Wiley & Sons.

Eurich, Tasha. 2017. *Insight: Why We're Not as Self-aware as We Think, and How Seeing Ourselves Clearly Helps Us Succeed at Work and in Life.* New York: Crown Business.

Hesse, Hermann. 2017. *Demian.* London, England: Penguin Classics.

Kashdan Todd B., David Disabato, Fallon Goodman and Patrick McKnight. "The Five-Dimensional Curiosity Scale Revised (5DCR): Briefer Subscales While Separating Overt and Covert Social Curiosity." *Personality and Individual Differences,* April 2020. https://doi.org/10.1016/j.paid.2020.109836.

Lievens, Filip, Spencer H. Harrison, Patrick Mussel, and Jordan A. Litman. "Killing the Cat? A Review of Curiosity at Work." *Academy of Management Annals. January 2022. https://doi.org/10.5465/annals.2020.0203.*

MLA. Laozi. 1972. *Tao Te Ching.* New York: Vintage Books.

Nhat Hanh, Thich. 2017. *The Art of Living.* New York: Harper One.

Rodenhizer, Samuel. "I Don't Like That Man. I Must Get to Know Him Better (ABRAHAM LINCOLN)." February 18, 2019. https://quotationcelebration.wordpress.com/2019/02/18/i-dont-like-that-man-i-must-get-to-know-him-better-abraham-lincoln/.

SurveyMonkey. "2020 research report: How to adapt and thrive in times of crisis: New Insights on How Agility and Curiosity Are Helping Organizations Weather the Storm of 2020." SurveyMonkey research report, 2020. https://www.surveymonkey.com/mp/2020-research-report/.

Yestobeatrice. *George Eastman "The Wizard of Photography" Documentary* (Part 2/3). July 21, 2015. Video, 18:18. https://www.youtube.com/watch?v=RwwWO6iqkUg.

PART 2

CHAPTER 5

Berlyne Daniel E. "Curiosity and Learning." *Motivation and Emotion*. Volume 2, Number 2, 1978.

Dixon, Matthew, and Brent Adamson. 2011. *The Challenger Sale: Taking Control of the Customer Conversation*. New York: Portfolio/Penguin.

Eurich, Tasha. "Increase Your Self-awareness with One Simple Fix." Filmed November 2017 at TEDxMileHigh. TEDx video. 17:18.
https://www.ted.com/talks/tasha_eurich_increase_your_self_awareness_with_one_simple_fix?language=en.

Gelb, David (creator). *Chef's Table*. Volume 3, Episode 6. "Virgilio Martinez." Accessed September 12, 2021. Netflix.

Gruber, Matthias J., Ashvanti Valji, and Charan Ranganath. 2019. *The Cambridge Handbook of Motivation and Learning: Curiosity and Learning: A Neuroscientific Perspective*. Cambridge: Cambridge University Press.
https://orca.cardiff.ac.uk/123206/1/R1_Curiosity_Chapter_submitted.pdf.

Merck KGaA, Darmstadt, Germany, Group Communication. *Merck: State of Curiosity Report 2018*.
https://www.merckgroup.com/company/en/State-of-Curiosity-Report-2018-International.pdf.

Shankar, Gurudev Sri Sri Ravi. *If You Have Prejudice You Can't Call Yourself a Scientist*. Video, 25:14. Premiered Oct 15, 2019. Accessed August 10, 2021.
https://www.youtube.com/watch?v=qbXYNOzqzlg.

The World's 50 Best Restaurants, "The World's 50 Best Restaurants List." Accessed December 12, 2021.
https://www.theworlds50best.com/list/1-50.

CHAPTER 6

Davis, Euan, and Manoj Mathew. 2019. *The Renaissance of Blue-Collar Work: Advanced Technologies Will Continue to Boost Conventional Blue-Collar Workers into Tech-enabled, High-skilled, Value-generating Roles*. Teaneck: Cognizant Center for the Future of Work.

Evans, Farrell. "How Nelson Mandela Used Rugby as a Symbol of South African Unity." July 29, 2021.
https://www.history.com/news/nelson-mandela-1995-rugby-world-cup-south-african-unity.

Gino, Francesca. "The Business Case for Curiosity." *Harvard Business Review*, September 2018.
https://hbr.org/2018/09/the-business-case-for-curiosity.

Harrison Spencer, "Your Super Power Curiosity." *The Curious Advantage Podcast*, produced by Paul Ashcroft, Simon Brown and Garrick Jones. Podcast, MP3 audio, 50:00. April 29, 2021.
https://podcasts.apple.com/cz/podcast/your-superpower-curiosity-the-curious-advantage-podcast/id1509018267?i=1000519222390.

Harrison Spencer, and Jon Cohen. *Curiosity Is Your Super Power.* Filmed in September 2018 at TedxLosGatos in Los Gatos, California, USA. Video, 17:29.
https://www.ted.com/talks/spencer_harrison_jon_cohen_curiosity_is_your_super_power.

Hofstede, Geert. "National Cultures Revisited." *Behavior Science Research* Vol. 18, No. 4 (1983): p: 285-305.
https://doi.org/10.1177/106939718301800403.

Loewenstein, George. "The Psychology of Curiosity." *Psychological Bulletin* vol. 116. No. 1 (1994): 75-98.

Merck KGaA, Group Communication. Merck: State of Curiosity Report 2016.
https://www.merckgroup.com/company/curiosity/Curiosity_Full-Report_English.pdf.

Moore, Richard. "The Conventional—But Peculiar—World of Executive Recruitment." Linkedin Article. September 8, 2021.
https://www.linkedin.com/pulse/conventionalbut-peculiar-world-executive-recruitment-richard-moore/.

Moss, Steve. "Taking the Risk Out of New Executive Hires." *Executive Springboard (blog).* December 15, 2017.
https://www.execspringboard.com/blog/taking-the-risk-out-of-new-executive-hires.

CHAPTER 7

Duhigg, Charles. "What Google Learned from Its Quest to Build the Perfect Team." *New York Times*, February 25, 2016.
https://www.nytimes.com/2016/02/28/magazine/what-google-learned-from-its-quest-to-build-the-perfect-team.html.

Tellegen Auke, David T. Lykken, Thomas J. Bouchard, Jr., Kimberly J. Wilcox, Nancy L. Segal, and Stephen Rich. "Personality Similarity in Twins Reared Apart and Together." *Journal of Personality and Social Psychology.* Vol. 54, No. 6 (1988). 1031-1039.
http://dx.doi.org/10.1037/0022-3514.54.6.1031.

Woolley, Anita Williams, Christopher F. Chabris, Alex Pentland, Nada Hashmi, and Thomas W. Malone. "Evidence for a Collective Intelligence Factor in the Performance of Human Groups."

Science Vol. 330, No. 6004(2010): 686-8. DOI: 10.1126/science.1193147.

CHAPTER 8

Encyclopedia Britannica Online. "Chernobyl disaster." Accessed September 17, 2021.
https://www.britannica.com/event/Chernobyl-disaster.

Gino, Francesca. "The Business Case for Curiosity." *Harvard Business Review*, September 2018.
https://hbr.org/2018/09/the-business-case-for-curiosity.

Hoffman, Reid. "95. Microsoft's Satya Nadella: Why we need re-founders." August 21, 2021. In *Masters of Scale with Reid Hoffman* Podcast. MP3 audio. 37 minutes.
https://podcasts.apple.com/us/podcast/masters-of-scale-with-reid-hoffman/id1227971746?i=1000533845297.

Hunt John. 2009. *The Art of the Idea*. New York: PowerHouse Books.

SurveyMonkey Inc. "Agility and Curiosity: Two Crucial Characteristics Found in Businesses Best Positioned to Survive the Pandemic." Research report. September 15, 2020.
https://www.surveymonkey.com/resources/premium/2020-research-report/.

PART 3

CHAPTER 9

Anonymous. "The S-Curve Pattern of Innovation: A Full Analysis." *Future Business Tech* (blog). April 20, 2021.
https://www.futurebusinesstech.com/blog/the-s-curve-pattern-of-innovation-a-full-analysis.

Eichenwald, Kurt. "Microsoft's Lost Decade." *Vanity Fair.* July 24, 2012.
http://www.vanityfair.com/news/business/2012/08/microsoft-lost-mojo-steve-ballmer.

Harrison, Spencer. "Your Super Power Curiosity." *The Curious Advantage Podcast*, Produced by Paul Ashcroft, Simon Brown and Garrick Jones, April 29, 2021.
https://podcasts.apple.com/cz/podcast/your-superpower-curiosity-the-curious-advantage-podcast/id1509018267?i=1000519222390.

Merck KGaA, Group Communication. cite: Merck: State of Curiosity Report 2018.
https://www.merckgroup.com/company/en/State-of-Curiosity-Report-2018-International.pdf.

Meyer, Ron, and Ronald Meyers. 2013. *Sovereign or Servant*. Rotterdam: Center for Strategy and Leadership.
https://www.c4sl.eu/wp-content/uploads/2015/06/sovereign_or_servant-1.pdf.

CHAPTER 10

Boston Consulting Group. "Overcoming the Innovation Readiness Gap." April 2021. (https://web-assets.bcg.com/bc/fe/f74e5e0d48e3b36a15a0c016c354/bcg-most-innovative-companies-2021-apr-2021-v5.pdf).

Mantle, Mickey. 1964. *The Quality of Courage*. Garden City, New York: Doubleday.

Marrow, Alexander. "We're a Tech Company." *Reuters.* September 24, 2020.
https://www.reuters.com/article/us-russia-sberbank-technology-focus-idUSKCN26F13Q.

Sberbank. "Sber Presents Development Strategy 2023." Sberbank Corporate Website. November 30, 2020. https://www.sberbank.com/news-and-media/press-releases/article?newsID=52848c66-9deb-4d8d-ac56-d3b4586d2667&blockID=7&regionID=77&lang=en&type=NEWS.

CHAPTER 11

Berne, Eric. 1972. *What Do You Say After You Say Hello?* New York: Grove Press, Inc.

Gruber, Matthias J., Ashvanti Valji, and Charan Ranganath. 2019. *The Cambridge Handbook of Motivation and Learning: Curiosity and Learning: A Neuroscientific Perspective.* Cambridge: Cambridge University Press. https://orca.cardiff.ac.uk/123206/1/R1_Curiosity_Chapter_submitted.pdf.

McCracken, Harry. "How Gmail Happened: The Inside Story of Its Launch Ten Years Ago." *Time Magazine.* April 1, 2014. https://time.com/43263/gmail-10th-anniversary/.

Murphy, Bill, Jr. "Google Says It Still Uses the '20-Percent Rule,' and You Should Totally Copy It." *Inc. Magazine,* November 1, 2020. https://www.inc.com/bill-murphy-jr/google-says-it-still-uses-20-percent-rule-you-should-totally-copy-it.html.

Schrage, Michael. "Just How Valuable Is Google's "20% Time"?" *Harvard Business Review,* August 20, 2013. https://hbr.org/2013/08/just-how-valuable-is-googles-2-1.

CHAPTER 12

Gartner. "Gartner Says Only 20 Percent of Employees Have the Skills Needed For Both Their Current Role And Their Future Career." Gartner corporate website. September 6, 2018. https://www.gartner.com/en/newsroom/press-releases/2018-09-06-gartner-says-only-20-percent-of-employees-have-the-skills-needed-for-both-their-current-role-and-their-future-career.

Lagravenese, Richard Dir. *The Freedom Writers' Diary.* MTV Films 2007. Netflix.

CHAPTER 13

Anonymous. "Xiaomi Phone Teaser Leaves Much to the Imagination, Save for Its Lack of Girth." Avianet.com. January 13, 2015. https://www.aivanet.com/2015/01/xiaomi-phone-teaser-leaves-much-to-the-imagination-save-for-its-lack-of-girth/.

Big Buck (jdryznar). "Favor From Clever Dudes." *LiveJournal* (blog), March 4, 2002. Accessed October 22, 2021. https://jdryznar.livejournal.com/64477.html?00cf6878).

Galbraith, John Kenneth, quoted in *The Guardian*. London: 28 July 1989. Quoted in: Burgers, Willem. 2008. *Marketing Revealed: Challenging the Myths*. New York: Palgrave MacMillan.

Hinchliffe, Mark. "World's Oldest, Roman Holiday Vespa Sells." *Motorbike News*. March 29, 2017.

Huddleston, Tom, Jr. "Netflix Didn't Kill Blockbuster—How Netflix Almost Lost the Movie Rental Wars. September 22, 2020. Accessed September 2, 2021. https://www.cnbc.com/2020/09/22/how-netflix-almost-lost-the-movie-rental-wars-to-blockbuster.html.

Jurberg, Ash. "7 Product Placements We Still Talk About Years Later." *Better Marketing*. Jun 30, 2020. https://bettermarketing.pub/7-product-placements-we-still-talk-about-years-later-6144ef43c1fc.

PART 4

CHAPTER 14

Bedford, Susannah. "Growth Mindset and Motivation." *Research Papers in Education,* Vol. 32 No. 4(2017): 424-443. DOI: 10.1080/02671522.2017.1318809.

Fogg, BJ. 2020. *TINY HABITS: The Small Changes That Change Everything.* 1st ed., London, Penguin Random House UK.

Goldsmith, Marshall, and Mark Reiter. 2007. *What Got You Here Won't Get You There: How Successful People Become Even More Successful.* New York, NY: Hyperion.

Nova, Nicolas. "'Question Your Teaspoons." *Nicolas Nova* (blog). January 10, 2008. http://www.nicolasnova.net/pasta-and-vinegar/2008/01/10/question-your-tea-spoons.

Quartz. *How Bill Gates Remembers What He Reads.* Video. 2:12. Premiered February 12, 2019. Accessed July 2, 2021. https://www.youtube.com/watch?v=8xwh88cI_d8.

Zeng, Guang, Hanchao Hou, and Kaiping Peng. "Effect of Growth Mindset on School Engagement and Psychological Well-Being of Chinese Primary and Middle School Students: The Mediating Role of Resilience." *Frontiers in Psychology,* 29 November 2016. https://doi.org/10.3389/fpsyg.2016.01873.

ACKNOWLEDGMENTS

Thank you to everyone who has been a part of my journey writing *The Workplace Curiosity Manifesto*. There is no way such a blessing would have been realized without your encouragement, guidance, and support.

First, I'd like to thank my family for walking by my side in n this journey every step of the way. From the moment I left a cushy corporate job and created the Global Curiosity Institute to the grueling task of revising my whole manuscript and all the steps in-between, I'm grateful for my wife, Jeltje, and my children, Rik, Femke, Koen, and Menko for the numerous discussions around our big, round dinner table over the years and more recently for allowing me to indulge in my daily writing exercise. Without your daily support from the beginning, I would never have felt comfortable climbing the strenuous path to publishing this book.

I am grateful to my mom, who was probably my greatest supporter in this journey and wanted to be the first one to order it. She encouraged me already early in life to take the road less traveled. She and my late father gave me the space to explore myself and the world. They were fine with me traveling across Europe all by myself when I was only seventeen and kept me out of school to simply join them when visiting art exhibitions. They accepted me for who I was and made sure I retained my childhood curiosity.

Second, to all the people whose stories I share in my book. Your bravery in being vulnerable, your insights, and your gracefulness in spending time with me to tell your story have been inspiring. You helped me in creating a much richer story by sharing deep insights on the role of curiosity in your organizations, the psychology or philosophy underpinning it, or specific research you are doing in this space. I thank you for your ideas and your generosity. You have given me enough information to fill several books. You are all my heroes.

Adrian Stäubli	Elizabeth McManus
Alex Evans	Elliott Masie
Alexandre Santille	Fredrik Östbye
Alison Horstmeyer	Henriette Fink
Bror Sachsberg	Jordy Kool
Carl Naughton	Jürgen Heyman
Charlie Whyman	Kris Van Assche
Christine Blum-Heuser	Kurt Verweire
Clara Cecchini	Lars Spicker Olesen
Clark Quinn	Lori Niles-Hofmann
Donald H Taylor	Martijn Rademakers
Edward D. Hess	Mervi Palander

Mike Pino

Nick Shackleton-Jones

Nick van Dam

Nicolas Alaerts

Niklas Lindholm

Nina Wittmer

Oliver Kempkens

Perry Timms

Rob Ferrone

Simon Brown

Soren Meibom

Teddy Frank

Todd Kashdan

Ulrik Juul Christensen

Uwe Ohl

Vincent-Pierre Giroux

Willem Burgers

Wout van Impe

Yury Boshyk

Third, I want to thank the very generous group of individuals who purchased one or more copies of this book during the pre-sale. You are the ones who made the publication of this story possible. Thank you for making an investment in my story and my writing. Several of you took part in beta-reading the manuscript. I was not sure what to think of inviting all of you to become critics of the manuscript, yet, boy, was it worth it. Your reflections, nudges, and feedback helped me lift the book to a whole new level. For this, I am truly grateful.

Aadharsh Rao

Aaron D. Preston

Aarthi Ramesh

Ade Derbyshire-Moore

Adriana Cleves

Ajmal Noorani

Akshat Sharma

Alan Glasspool

Albers Retail

Albert Hietink

Alberto Gonzalez Otero

Alexandre Santille

Amit Garg

Ammar Al-Madhagi

Andrew Lax

Angelina Andrew

Anil Santhapuri

Anjana Sonal Minj

Anna Willems

Antarpreet Singh

Arto Vainiomäki

Ashish Arora

Asma Afreen

Balesh Raghurajan

Barry Byrne

Bart Lambrecht

Beatriz Perez-Soto

Bernard Melendez

Bidisha Banerjee

Bijoy Venugopal

Brian Tietje

Buck Seward

Carla Compagno

Carlos Agustin

Catalina Schveninger

Celeste Stewart

Charles Paré

Charu Pokhriyal

Chelsea Marti

Christine Dauchez

Ciara Duffy

Clare Inkster

Cristian Arguello

D Dharmendra

Danielle Hautaniemi

Debasis Dutta

Deepak Arora

Delphine Lefrère

Detlef Hold

Devendra Naik

Dinesh Ravindran

Divya Pareek

Dominik Rus

Duncan Dunlop

Dushyant Kumar Pandey

Elizabeth McManus

Elke van Hooydonk

Elsje Peletier

Ena Voute

Eric Koester

Eric Saint-Gelais

Erik-Hans Munnik

Eskil Berg Kappel

Ewa Hutmacher

Ewa Wisniewska

Fernando Cuevas G

Flore Segalen

Florence Meyer

Gideon Lopes Cardozo

Goran Folkesson

Graham Blair

Gurpinder Sidhu

Gurpreet Kalra

Han Van Der Pool

Hans Conijn

Hans Dirkzwager

Harmen Dubbelaar

Harpreet Kanwar

Harshavardhan Raja

Hector Garcia

Heidi Vandousselaere

Henriette Wesselink

Henrik Waitz

Hubert Renson

Huw Newton-Hill

Ido Shikma

Ignaz Worm

Ivor Williamson

Jaap Schuuring

Jacobus van 't Riet

Jagannath VMD

James Jeude

Jane Piper

Janine Adrien

Jason Fredrick van Eunen

Jeltje Peletier

Jitendra C. Putcha

John Rhodes

Joke de Groote

Joseph Errold Melvin

Jyothi Mani

Karen Ferris

Kari Kangas

Karn Singh

Kathelijne Hofkens

Katja Schipperheijn

Khurram Jamil

Kinyanjui Kombani

Kishore Krishnan

Krishnan Nilakantan

Krishnan Unni

Kristoff Temmerman

Kshitij Nerurkar

Lori Niles-Hofmann

Lucy Jakupi-Haugen

Madhav Dhasmana

Manjunath Kygonahally

Marcia Platilha

Margaret McNulty

Marie Francine Avasilencei

Menko Deroos

Mercedes María Castiñeiras
Vilariño

Michael Frechette

Michael Gaffney

Michael Hernandez

Mike Pino

Mille von Appen Hertz

Mine Kobal

Miriam Dumaine

Misha Akbar

Mridul Kaushik

Munmun Kc

Murali Palani

Nabamita Chatterjee

Natalie Turner

Navin Kumar

Neha Verma

Nezir Vragovic

Nikhil Chadha

Nilanjana Pal

Nils Junge

Niranjan Kulkarni

Noe Gutierrez

Pascal Anene

Paul Arnold

Paul Pan

Pieter Peletier

Prarthana Alley

Pratap Gopalakrishnan

Pratyusha Sharma

Rachel Wilson Rugelsjøen

Raf Lamberts

Raghav Chakravarthy

Rahul Bhatt

Raj Dharmaraj

Rajeev PM

Ramanand JR

Ramesh Ramachandran

Ravi Kaklasaria

Rein Hintzen

Renske Valk

Richard Coote

Robert Byssz

Robert Danna

Robert David

Rohit Gupta

Ronald Plantinga

Ronald Van der Molen

Ruud Wilgenkamp

Sakthivel Rajasekar

Sambit Dash

Samir Malhotra

Sanjani palani

Sanjib Basu

Saransh Agrawal

Sean Kennedy

Shalini Sunder

Shanil Sathya Seelan

Sharath Baburaj

Sharon Lamm-Hartman

Shyam Sundar

Sreehari Vimala Sreekantan

Sridhar Iyer

Srinivas Peri

Stefan Marose

Stephanie Auping

Stephen Jesukanth Martin

Stephen Krempl

Sunil Deshmukh

Sunil Tatkar

Suresh Kumar DN

Tamal Bhattacharya

Tanis Marquette

Taylor Blake

Tayseer Almattar

Teddy Frank

Teena George

Thiruvenkateshwaran
Ramachandran

Tim Smits

Tom Deurloo

Tom Haak

Ulrik Juul Christensen

Vanessa Janssen

Vas Theodorakis

Venkatesh Sanem

Victorien van Manen

Vijayanand Bhoopalan

Vijoy Basu

Ville Pellinen

Vincent-Pierre Giroux

Wei Jing Ho

Willem Burgers

William J. Ryan

William Pasmore

Willy de Jong

Wim van Hennekeler

Wouter Koetzier

Yvonne Newlands

Fourth, to all the people who helped me in polishing my thoughts and reflections on the power of curiosity. I am thinking of all the colleagues I had the honor of working with. I am also thinking of all the participants in my curiosity workshops and sessions who triggered deeper reflection because of your curious questions. Because of those workshops, I was able to collect data, helping me to write this book and measure curiosity.

Lastly, and probably most importantly, I must thank the teams at New Degree Press and the Creator Institute for their hard work in supporting me on my publishing journey. To my editors: Rachel Welsch, Janice Riley, and Kate Victory Hannisian, your patience, kindness, and wisdom were instrumental in getting my manuscript to publishing; thank you. I owe a debt of gratitude to Eric Koester of the Creator Institute and Georgetown University for his encouragement and coaching. Without you, Eric, I would not have had the confidence to get started in the first place.

Printed in Germany
by Amazon Distribution
GmbH, Leipzig